Anastasia

by Marcelle Maurette

English Adaptation by
Guy Bolton

A SAMUEL FRENCH ACTING EDITION

SAMUEL FRENCH

FOUNDED 1830

New York Hollywood London Toronto

SAMUELFRENCH.COM

ANASTASIA was first presented by Elaine Perry at the Lyceum Theatre, New York City, on December 20, 1954, with the following cast:

(In Order of Appearance)

CHERNOV .... *Boris Tumarin*
VARYA............................... *Sefton Darr*
PETROVIN .... *David J. Stewart*
PRINCE BOUNINE .... *Joseph Anthony*
SERGEI .... *William Callaln*
ANNA .... *Viveca Lindfors*
COUNSELLOR DRIVINITZ .... *Carl Low*
SLEIGH DRIVER .... *Stuart Garmain*
CHARWOMAN .... *Vivian Nathan*
DR. SERENSKY .... *Michael Strong*
DOWAGER EMPRESS............... *Eugenie Leontovich*
BARONESS LIVENBAUM................ *Dorothy Patten*
PRINCE PAUL .... *Hurd Hatfield*

SCENES

The action of the play takes place in Prince Bounine's house on the outskirts of Berlin.

ACT ONE

January, 1926

ACT TWO

One month later.

ACT THREE

Three weeks later.

Anastasia

ACT ONE

SETTING: *Bounine's home: A house on the outskirts of Berlin, 1926. This is a room which, when we first see it, is used as an office.*

A platform runs from the Right wall to the Left wall—the entire width of the stage with three steps down to the front area.

Up Right Center in the back wall is a small door leading downstairs to the cellar and out to the rear entrance of the house. Up Left Center in the back wall is a double door leading to what will be known ater at Anna's room. In the up Left wall is a double door leading to the hall and front entrance of the house. Also in the Left wall lis a large double window, the downstage one of which is practical. There is a window seat in front of the window. The entire window is boarded up from the outside.

Down Right is a larfie crate with vodka, brandy, glasses, matches, cigarettes, ashtray and a box of candy on it. Leaning on this crate are two small pictures. Leaning on the Right wall above the crate are two larger pictures. Up Right in the angle between the back wall and the Right wall is another crate. Leaning against the stage Right side are two packages of books. On the crate are a stack of books, a filing cabinet with two drawers and three photo albums. On the upstage wall between the doors is a life-size poster of a female figure in court dress with crown on head. The face is blank. To the Left of the poster tacked to the wall is a picture of the grand

*duchess Anastasia, from which the poster has
been copied. Also Left of poster is a small cross
attached to the wall. On the floor Left of the poster
is a jar of water-color brushes. Right Center is an
armchair (on stage floor backed up against the first
steps), with a woman's gaily colored hat hung on
the back. Left Center is an oval wicker table with
two old chairs—one up stage and one Right of table,
and a stool below to Left. On the table are circulars
printed in Russian, some with a photograph on them.
Also on the table are a typewriter, an account book,
a book file with papers, cigarettes, matches, ash
tray, pencil and an old-fashioned goose-neck lamp.
Down Left is another crate with circulars on it. All
three crates are marked "Oben-Vorsichet-Nicht
Sturtzen," and the like. A large chandelier hangs
Center. It is not lit.*

*The stage is dimly lit. MOONLIGHT streams through
the cracks in the boarded-up window. The goose-neck
throws a glow over the table and the surrounding area
and a dim LIGHT comes through the front door from
the hallway.*

CHEROV *is sitting Right of table typing and check-
ing figures in the account book. The time is almost
11 P.M. He writes in ledger. As he starts typing
again—*

DOORBELL rings.

CHERNOV *crosses up toward the front door.*

DOORBELL.

CHERNOV *stops and crosses to door up Right
center.*

DOORBELL.

CHERNOV. *(Calling off)* Varya!
VARYA. *(Off.)* Coming!

(CHERNOV *crosses and sits Right of table again.* VARYA
*enters and crosses to front door. Ad lib in hall be-
tween* VARYA *and* PETROVIN.)

PETROVIN. He's not at home?

VARYA. No, but your friend is inside.

PETROVIN. This house is cold. You need a stove. *(He appears on platform with VARYA as he says this.)* Maybe I'd better draw one on the wall, one of our big Russian pechkas.

(VARYA *exits up Right Center.*)

Ah, Chernov: Greetings! (PETROVIN *crosses down to* CŒERNOV.)

CHERNOV. Good evening.

PETROVIN. The servant tells me the Prince is not here *(Crosses to table for cigarette.)*

CHERNOV. No, I've been waiting for half an hour. I've spent the time drawing up a summary of our accounts. It's not a pleasant picture. The Prince has been horribly extravagant.

PETROVIN. Surely a Prince is entitled to live in a house of this size?

CHERNOV. *(Rising)* It isn't the house, it's what goes on in it—the champagne suppers—this: *(Crossing to armchair Right Center, he holds up woman's hat.)*

PETROVIN. *(Crossing to Center)* Oh, that—he's so Russian!

CHERNOV. I'm a Russian, too, but I live in one room in a cheap hotel.

PETROVIN. Without any women's hats. *(Crosses Right to crate for candy.)*

CHERNOV. Yes, look at all these crates—filled with expensive furnishings.

PETROVIN. *(Sitting Right Center)* He's used to living with beautiful things. His villa in the Crimea was a delight. The Soviets have turned it into an orphan asylum.

CHERNOV. To which the Prince probably contributed one or two orphans.

PETROVIN. Do you know why he sent for us to come here tonight?

CHERNOV. *(Crossing to front door)* No, he merely said he wanted us here at ten o'clock. *(Looks at watch.)* It's now almost eleven.

PETROVIN. He loves to be mysterious.

(CHERNOV *peeks out door.*)

Perhaps he has come on some clue as to the whereabouts of that girl.

CHERNOV. I've followed up a dozen such clues. *(Crosses Center on platform.)* Do you think there ever was a girl who told those hospital nurses she was the Tsar's daughter?

PETROVIN. Are you suggesting His Excellency lied to us—his partners?

CHERNOV. *(Crossing down to Left of PETROVIN)* I'm only suggesting that lying is a thing in which His Excellency excels.

PETROVIN. *(Crosses Right, puts candy on crate and takes drink.)* The story was perfectly convincing, and it happened just at the time the rumors of Anastasia's miraculous escape were flying about the Russian colony.

CHERNOV. *(Following PETROVIN)* The timing of her appearance was, as you say, excellent—her disappearance, after no one but the Prince had seen her, was not quite so fortunate.

BOUNINE. *(Off.)* Sergei! Look after the lady—give her anything she wants.

(VARYA *enters; crosses to hall.*)

CHERNOV. *(Crosses Left of armchair.)* Women again!

BOUNINE. *(Appearing with VARYA)* Good evening, comrades—if that term doesn't grate too unpleasantly on your White Russian ears.

PETROVIN. *(Below armchair.)* Good evening, Excellency.

BOUNINE. *(Giving VARYA hat and gloves)*

(VARYA *closes door.*)

I'm sorry to have kept you waiting. I had an adventure—not what we usually mean by that expression, but still, J will admit, it involved a woman.

(VARYA *gives hat and gloves to CHERNOV and exits up Right Center.*)

CHERNOV. Petrovin and I are wondering why you sent for us.

BOUNINE. Do you feel a strange warmth at the back of your necks? *(Crosses down Center.)* It may be the hot breath of disaster. *(Crosses Right for drink.)* Gentlemen, we have run into trouble.

PETROVIN. Trouble? What sort of trouble?

BOUNINE. *(Pouring drink)* Some of our subscribers have got together. They've formed a committee with that busybody Councillor Drivinitz at its head. They ordered me to meet them.

CHERNOV. What did you say to them?

BOUNINE. Nothing—I didn't go. It's clear enough what they were going to demand.

PETROVIN. That we produce the Grand Duchess Anastasia?

BOUNINE. And immediately too.

CHERNOV. *(Crosses Left, puts hat and gloves on table.)* I've been expecting this to happen.

BOUNINE. *(At Right of armchair.)* Don't forget it's more than three months since we sent out our appeals for help.

CHERNOV. *(Crossing Center)* Once the girl disappeared, we should have given the thing up— *(Crosses Left, below table, to above window.)* Sent our investors back their money.

PETROVIN. *(Crosses Left, takes typewriter from table, puts it on crate down Left.)* If they are really closing in on us, we had better divide up what's left and celar out of Berlin.

(CHERNOV *crosses down Left.*)

BOUNINE. *(Sits armchair.)* I don't believe we'd get very far.

PETROVIN. *(Crossing to above table and gathering cir culars)* But if we stay here, we'll end up in prison.

CHERNOV. *(Sitting stool Left)* A German prison!

PETROVIN. A Russian one is bad enough.

CHERNOV. Russians are sloppy and inefficient even as

barbarians. These Germans use their convicts for medical experiments.

PETROVIN. *(Turning to* BOUNINE) Is that true? I need a drink.

BOUNINE. Over there.

PETROVIN. *(Crossing Right to crate)* Why did I ever get myself into this? Why? Why?

CHERNOV. *(Following to Center)* You went into it for the same reason I did—you needed the money.

PETROVIN. Want some?

CHERNOV. My gallstones— *(Crossing to above table.)* Conspiracy to defraud—what's the penalty? How long? Does anyone know?

(PETROVIN *sits on steps below crate up Right.)*

BOUNINE. Don't despair, my friends, perhaps we're not beaten yet.

CHERNOV. *(Sits on chair above table.)* Not beaten? We're called on to produce a murdered princess—

BOUNINE. What would you say to a miracle? It seems the appropriate moment for one.

CHERNOV. What do you mean?

BOUNINE. I wanted you to digest my bad news before telling you my good. *(Rises; crosses up Center to poster.)* Gentlemen, I have found her, at the eleventh hour, I have found her.

PETROVIN. *(Rises; to Right of armchair.)* Found her? Found who?

CHERNOV. Not your Anna Broun?

BOUNINE. Yes, the same Anan Broun I talked with that evening in the hospital at Dausdorf. *(Crosses down Center.)* The same Anna Broun who told one of the nuns that she was the daughter of Nicholas II.

PETROVIN. *(Crossing to* BOUNINE) Where did you find her?

BOUNINE. *(Sitting Right of table)* I was sure I had caught a glimpse of her the other day when I was driving through the Riemstrasse. The woman turned into a side street and before I had a chance to tell Sergei to follow her, she had disappeared.—Tonight, under the spur of this threat, I went back there. I made inquiries, promised a reward to anyone who would help me to find her and ran her down at last—where do you think?

PETROVIN. Where?

BOUNINE. On one of the bridges that crosses the Landwehr Canal. I had a notion she was thinking of throwing herself into it.

PETROVIN. Why?

BOUNINE. Ill, out of work, half-starved—

PETROVIN. Did she explain why she ran away from the hospital after you promised to help to find her family?

BOUNINE. I'm afraid she didn't trust me. I don't think she does now.

CHERNOV. And what is your opinion now that you have seen her again? Of her claim, I mean?

BOUNINE. Precisely what it was before. She is no more the Grand Duchess than I am one of the murdered Grand Dukes.

CHERNOV. If she's as unconvincing as that what makes you think Drivinitz and his friends will accept her?

BOUNINE. It's not for nothing that those hospntal nuns had faith in her story. You see, there are certain features about her.

CHERNOV. Has she anything to back it up with? Any papers or family heirlooms?

BOUNINE. Nothing. And she's not backing it up.

PETROVIN. What do you mean?

BOUNINE. She now says that the story she told the nuns was a lot of nonsense. That she isn't the Tsar's daughter.

PETROVIN. *(Crosses Right to armchair and sits.)* But, good God, if she denies it herself, what hope—?

BOUNINE. She'll come back to it. She's a bit unbalanced. Her story today is that she doesn't know who she is, and I daresay that's true.

CHERNOV. *(Rises; to Left, above table.)* An amnesiac?

BOUNINE. That certainly, and at times a prey to all sorts

of bizarre fancies. In her vague state, however, she's all the more ready to receive impressions. I'll *make* her play our little charade—

PETROVIN. And if she can't play it?

BOUNINE. If she makes a mess of it, we can still point a finger at her. She is the guilty one. We are only her poor innocent dupes whom she deceived with her lies.

CHERNOV. *(Crossing back to* BOUNINE*)* That way she might save us from a charge of fraud.

PETROVIN. *(Rises; to Center.)* And this time are we to be taken to see the girl?

BOUNINE. Of course you're going to see her. What do you say—shall we have her in now?

PETROVIN. You mean to say she's here?

BOUNINE. In the servants' hall—

(PETROVIN *crosses and opens front doors.)*

with Sergei standing guard. (BOUNINE *rises; crosses to door.)* I told him to get her some food. She seemed badly in need of it. *(Calling off)* Sergei, bring the girl in here.

(CHERNOV *closes window and board.)*

SERGEI. *(Off.)* Yes, Excellency.

(PETROVIN *takes* BOUNINE'S *overcoat; puts it on crate up Right.)*

BOUNINE. *(Crossing to below armchair)* Let me caution you, don't speak to her in Russian. She says she doesn't understand it.

CHERNOV. What? But that makes it impossible.

BOUNINE. It's a lie. She has a definite Slavic accent. Don't worry, I'll break her down.

PETROVIN. *(Crossing down Right of* BOUNINE*)* I remember hearing tales of your cigarette ends. Berlin isn't Russia.

BOUNINE. If I should fail we'll have to picture it as some

Freudian quirk a defensive reaction born of her long, under-cover journey.

CHERNOV. You think they'll swallow that?

(As he speaks, SERGEI *appears shepherding* ANNA. SERGEI *gives her a slight push.)*

SERGEI. Go on in.

BOUNINE. Yes, come in, Fraulein. I want you to meet my friends.

(ANNA hesitates for a moment, then comes down. She grasps at Left Center chairback for support. SERGEI exits, closing door.)

Take a seat.

(ANNA sinks into chair.)

A glass of vodka?

ANNA. Thank you.

(BOUNINE gestures to PETROVIN, who brings drink from crate down Right. CHERNOV takes off overcoat and puts it on crate down Left.)

BOUNINE. *(Taking glass from PETROVIN and giving it to ANNA)* These are the gentlemen I spoke of. I am putting you in their hands. *(Crosses Left of table.)* They are going to examine you.

ANNA. Examine? Are they doctors?

BOUNINE. *(Crossing to above table)* No, you won't have to undress. Just allow them to look at you.

ANNA. Oh, is that all? May I smoke?

BOUNINE. *(Taking glass from ANNA and putting it on table—puts cigarette in her mouth.)* Help yourself. When you and I talked just now, I promised you employment. These two associates of mine wish to determine how well you fit our requirements.

(BOUNINE crosses below table to crate down Left. PETROVIN strikes a match and holds it, lighting her cigarette. CHERNOV moves forward, both MEN staring

down at her. PETROVIN *is Right of* ANNA, CHERNOV
at her Left.)

CHERNOV. To begin with, the eyes—
PETROVIN. The eyes are right.
CHERNOV. Where did you see the eyes of the—other?
PETROVIN. *(Rising)* It was at Notre Dame de Kazan
in 1915 when we had been driven back by Hindenburg.
She came to the church to pray with her mother, and they
placed a candle before the big ikon. *(Crosses Left to*
BOUNINE, *below table.)* I saw two little candles reflected
in her eyes.
CHERNOV. Blue eyes?
PETROVIN. *(Crossing back above table and sitting Left
of* ANNA) Blue-grey, with the two candle flames like a
pair of golden dots. And just now when I held the match
for this one's cigarette—I saw exactly the same thing.
Very few eyes will pick up a reflection like that. I'm an
artist. I know what I'm talking about.
CHERNOV. *(Crossing Right of* ANNA) What about the
mouth?
PETROVIN. All wrong—a drawn, taut mouth. *Hers*
smiled easily. Even at that solemn moment she smiled.
Her teeth were beautifully even, white and shiny. I was
so close I could smell the scent she was wearing.
CHERNOV. *(Crossing Center)* I hope it was nicer than
this one's.
BOUNINE. If that's all that's troubling you we can
easily perfume her. And, Piotr, let me suggest that a
mouth that smiled readily might not smile so much after
what she would have gone through.
CHERNOV. *(At armchair.)* What about the height? She
looks too tall to me.
BOUNINE. The last time she reviewed our regiment, I
remember as I held her stirrup to mount that the brim of
her kilpak was on the level of my eye.
CHERNOV. Stand up.
ANNA. What did you say?
CHERNOV. I said, "Stand up."

(PETROVIN *pulls* ANNA *to her feet.* ANNA *drops cigarette and picks it up.* PETROVIN *crosses up Left on platform and compares their heights.*)

PETROVIN. Of course she's eight years older than the other was—when she died. *(Takes photo from wall.)*

BOUNINE. And I must remind you again that those eight years would not have been what the first sixteen were.

CHERNOV. Go over there. I want to see how you walk. *(She turns, obeying him; walks slouchingly toward crate Right.* CHERNOV *laughs scornfully and crosses to above and Right of table.)*

They were taught to walk carrying a book on their heads —another thing we will have to tell our investors she has somehow forgotten.

PETROVIN. *(Crossing above to Right of* ANNA *and then below to Center)* Where is this resemblance that so impressed you? I don't see it. I don't see it at all.

(ANNA *is left by herself as the* TWO MEN *go over to* BOUNINE.)

CHERNOV. After all those awed descriptions we gave them—the Tsar's noble bearing, her mother's matchless complexion— And now we're to show them—this? *(Sits Right of table.)*

BOUNINE. *(Crossing to* CHERNOV *above table)* How have they seen the original? A white-clad figure in a rapidly moving carriage. Or one of a family group in the flowered stand at Krasnoie. Oh yes, they saw a great deal of her—*in the newspapers.*

(ANNA *lights cigarette, getting match on crate Right.*)

CHERNOV. What of the royal servants? There are still a few of them about.

BOUNINE. They'll see her through their tears, good faithful souls that they are.

CHERNOV. And the family?

(ANNA *turns Center.*)

BOUNINE. More serious, certainly. But it isn't as if there were a mother or a father to be dealt with. Or a brother and sisters. True, there is quit a wealth of uncles, aunts and cousins, despite the Bolsheviks and their firing squads. But they will refer secretly to their photographs, and as she will resemble those photographs—

(PETROVIN *crosses to* ANNA, *takes off her shawl and crosses back to Left and to above* CHERNOV.)

CHERNOV. *This* woman—?

(ANNA *crosses to armchair.*)

BOUNINE. Yes, I am sure by the time we are finished she'll be like—
        (PETROVIN *shows photo to* BOUNINE, *who waves it away.*)
–*very* like. Oh, it won't be the gay, pink-cheeked girl who danced in the Hall of Columns at the last ball ever held there.
        (ANNA *sits armchair.*)
But let us say she'll be as like as a dead body is to a living person.

CHERNOV. If we could present her to them lying in her coffin, it would be easier—no questions, no answers, no mistakes.

(PETROVIN *returns photo to wall Left of poster.*)

BOUNINE. *(Turning away Left)* A tempting idea, but you're forgetting the money.

CHERNOV. You surely don't believe you'll be able to convince the bankers?

BOUNINE. There's a chance. If we could get the family to accept her, the bankers would find it difficult to question their endorsement.

CHERNOV. When you said she would serve as a scapegoat, you were talking sense. Anything beyond that is hopeless.

BOUNINE. I don't agree. Anyway, let us try for the castle-in-the-air before settling for the cabin in the swamp.

CHERNOV (*Rising; to up Center.*) I admit you knew the original better than we did. I have studied the photographs in those albums we bought from the Grand Duke's lady friend and I can't see

BOUNINE. Get out the albums.

(PETROVIN *crosses to up Right crate for album.*)
They're here, aren't they? (*Crosses to Right of* ANNA.)

CHERNOV. I don't need to. I know them by heart. In the early ones she wore her hair down—there's one of her and her sister Olga dancing on the deck of a yacht. (*Crossing to Right of table*) In the more recent ones she appears heavier than her sisters, with stronger cheekbones—more Russian-looking.

PETROVIN. (*With album, crossing to Right of* CHERNOV) Yes, and then, at least for some of us, there is the final one— the one photographed by our imaginations.

CHERNOV. What are you talking about?

PETROVIN. In the cellar, where the murders were committed—she is standing up. her head and her hands she raised to shield it, pierced with bullets.

BOUNINE. Look at her hands.

(ANNA *appears to be asleep.* BOUNINE *takes cigarette from her hand and puts it on on down Right crate.*)

PETROVIN. What did you say?

BOUNINE. I said: "Look at her hands."

CHERNOV. You don't mean—?

BOUNINE. I told you there was a special feature— something rather surprising.

CHERNOV. Come here!

(She does not move. CHERNOV *goes to her.* PETROVIN *crosses and puts down album.)*
I said, "Come here."

(He catches hold of her arm. With a rough jerk, brings her over to light Right and above table. PETROVIN *catches her by the other arm.)*

PETROVIN. Open your hands.

BOUNINE. *(Crossing Center)* You'll find they are long and well-formed, with a scar in the middle. The hands of a crucified being.

PETROVIN. Yes, it's true.

BOUNINE. *(Crossing behind* ANNA *and pulling her into the chair)* And that isn't all. Look at her head, gentlemen.

(PETROVIN *shines lamp on* ANNA's *face.)*
The left temple—a long, narrow depression--the path of a bullet. *(Crosses above table to stool Left.)* Of course, it may be something more prosaic—a childhood accident—a rather bad one that caused a fracture— *(Sits stool.)*

CHERNOV. What is this scar? Is it from a bullet? Tell us.

ANNA. I don't remember.

CHERNOV. You don't remember how you got a wound like that? Of course you do. You're lying.

ANNA. There are many things I have forgotten.

(PETROVIN *replaces lamp.)*

CHERNOV. *(Crossing to* BOUNINE, *below table)* What are you going to say if they demand to see her immediately?

(ANNA *rises; to above chair—sees poster and crosses slowly to it.)*

PETROVIN. *(Above Left end of table.)* Yes, it will take time to teach her.

CHERNOV. "Time"? I should think so. Weeks, months. Years!

BOUNINE. I shall say that we've had her moved to a sanatorium in Switzerland which specializes in psychopathic amnesia.

PETROVIN. *(Turns and sees* ANNA.) Look!

BOUNINE. *(Rising)* It draws her like a magnet.

PETROVIN. *(Crossing to Left of* ANNA) Fraulein, turn around. Stand against the wall. Hold out your arms like this. *(Crossing to Left of* BOUNINE *at window)* She fits the figure exactly! I drew it from the record kept by the dressmaker.

(CHERNOV *crosses up to above Right end of table.)*

BOUNINE. *(Crossing up between* PETROVIN *and* CHERNOV) She's certainly the right height. That crown might be resting on her head.

ANNA. Let me go!

CHERNOV. What's the matter with you? Are you an epileptic?

BOUNINE. *(Crosses up Center on platform Left of* ANNA.) Come here. There's nothing holding you. *(He claps his hands in front of* ANNA's *face.)*
    (ANNA *turns and looks at poster.)*
You know who it is? It's yourself, Princess.

ANNA. *(Backing down Right Center, still looking at poster)* Don't call me "Princess."

BOUNINE. *(Following)* You told one of the nuns that you were Anastasia Nicholaevna, the daughter of the Tsar.

ANNA. *(Turns away and crosses down Right to crate.)* I was sick. When you are sick you get crazy ideas.

BOUNINE. Naturally, it's a thing you wish kept secret. You feel that if it were widely known, your life might be in danger.

ANNA. *(Turning to* BOUNINE) I made it up, I tell you. They asked me questions— "Who are you? Where do you come from? Who was your father?" Questions and questions—so I told them I was a royal princess. Lies! Lies! It isn't true!

BOUNINE. Stop it! Be quiet!

(DOORBELL rings.)

CHERNOV. Who's that? Who could be coming at this hour? *(Crosses up and peeks out front door.)*

DRIVINITZ. *(Off.)* I want to see Prince Bounine.

(Ad lib: SERGEI and DRIVINITZ, off.)

CHERNOV. *(Closing door and crossing Center on platform)* It's Drivinitz!

BOUNINE. *(Pushing ANNA upstage)* Quick, Chernov! Take her downstairs!

(As CHERNOV crosses to get ANNA, PETROVIN crosses above him to Right Center door and opens it.)

CHERNOV. *(Pulling ANNA up steps, through door)* Come!

ANNA. The cellar? That's where they were killed!

(PETROVIN slams door.)

BOUNINE. *(Sits in armchair.)* Quick, Piotro—get rid of that photograph!

    (PETROVIN hides photo behind poster, crosses to crate up Right and peers into one of the file drawers. KNOCK at door.)

Yes. Who is it?

SERGEI. *(Appearing in door)* Counsellor Drivinitz. Excellency.

BOUNINE. Show him in.

    (DRIVINITZ enters.)

Good evening, Counsellor. *(Rises; crosses up to DRIVINITZ on platform.)* Welcome to my somewhat disordered abode. I have only recently moved in here.

DRIVINITZ. So it appears. You needed more room,

(Takes off hat.) I suppose, for your account books and correspondence.

(BOUNINE *takes hat.*)

(DRIVINITZ *crosses down to table.)* The Anastasia Enterprise is prospering.

PETROVIN. Enterprise?

DRIVINITZ. *(Turning, scornfully)* Is this one of your partners?

BOUNINE. My friend, Petrovin, the artist.

DRIVINITZ. Artist, eh? *(Crossing to poster)* Then I take it, this is some of your work?

PETROVIN. *(To Right of poster.)* Yes, we are planning to have it reproduced for propaganda purposes.

DRIVINITZ. I notice the face is missing. It seems the clothes sat for you but not their owner.

BOUNINE. *(Crossing down Right Center and offering armchair, hanging hat on back of chair)* Her Imperial Highness has not been well enough to pose.

DRIVINITZ. *(Ignoring the offered chair and crossing to chcair Right of table)* It is evident that your fortunes have improved, Prince. It was not so long ago that you were driving a taxi. *(Sits.)* Now I see you riding about in a handsome car and giving expensive luncheon parties at the Adlon.

BOUNINE. *(Crosses to Right of* DRIVINITZ *and offers him a cigarette.)* I am conducting certain negotiations in the interest of the Grand Duchess; negotiations that will ultimately be of importance to you and the other investors.

DRIVINITZ. *(Ignoring the offer)* The "investors," as you call them, have reached the end of their patience. Some of us have asked you from time to time to produce evidence that the Princess Anastasia really exists and is in your care. We have been put off with vague replies and equally vague photographs.

BOUNINE. *(Crossing Left, above* DRIVINITZ, *to above table)* I have explained that the Princess is still very ill. Her doctors insist on isolation, rest, absolute quiet.

(CHERNOV *enters up Right Center and pauses on top step*

listening. Petrovin *moves to front of poster.)*

Drivinitz. My committee wishes to talk with her doctors.

Bounine. *(Crossing down Left of table)* I am sorry, but Her Highness is in a private sanitarium in Switzerland.

Drivinitz. *(Rising; to below table.)* I, for one, am ready to make the journey immediately.

Bounine. *(Meeting him below table)* My friends and I have just been discussing the advisability of bringing the Grand Duchess here to Berlin.

Chernov. *(Coming down a step)* That will, of course, take a little time—

(Drivinitz *turns.)*

Bounine. Allow me. Boris Chernov, formerly a banker.

Chernov. *(Crossing down to Right of* Drivinitz) A private establishment on the Nevsky Prospect, next door to the Cafe Ostrov.

(AD LIBS off: Anna *and* Varya.)

Drivinitz. What is that?

(Chernov *crosses up Center to second step and swings around, watching* Drivinitz.)

Petrovin. *(Crossing down to armchair and picking up woman's hat from back of chair)* Some ladies we were entertaining. One of them had a glass too many.

Bounine. *(Offers stool to* Drivinitz *and crosses above table to below and Left of* Chernov.) You had better go and see about it, Piotr.

(Chernov *continues his upstage movement to Left of Right Center door and opens it for* Petrovin.)

Petrovin. *(Crossing up, throws hat behind crate.)* Yes, certainly. If you'll excuse me

(BOUNINE *moves up Center.* BOUNINE *and* CHERNOV *are now on a line between* DRIVINITZ *and the cellar, with* PETROVIN *in the doorway.)*

BOUNINE. Perhaps I should explain. These are the two gentlemen who aided in the rescue of the Princess.
DRIVINITZ. A rescue from whom? And from where?
PETROVIN. Bucharest.

(Closes door behind him, with CHERNOV *speeding him on his way.)*

DRIVINITZ. *(Below Left end of table.)* Bucharest— really.
BOUNINE. *(Crossing to above armchair)*
  (CHERNOV *checks to see that front door is closed and crosses down Left to above window.)*
Yes, she was in hiding, afraid to tell anyone who she was —afraid even to admit that she was Russian. But Yourovski's execution squad had stamped her identification. She has the scar of a bullet wound along the left side of her head and another bullet—or possibly that same one —has pierced the palm of both hands.
DRIVINITZ. *(Crossing Center)* And why, may I ask, did you not come to the Russian Club this afternoon and tell us all this?
BOUNINE. Because I found the peremptory tone in which you summoned me insulting.
DRIVINITZ. There was good reason for us to adopt such a tone. We are convinced that we are being made the victims of a hoax.
BOUNINE. So you think all I have been telling you is a pack of lies?
DRIVINITZ. I think we were fools ever to have believed otherwise. The assassinations took place in 1918. This is 1926. Even a return from the dead should not take that long.
BOUNINE. Resurrections are a severe test of faith. There was a doubter named Thomas—

DRIVINITZ. And if this is a conspiracy, as I firmly believe, you have done an unforgivable thing, Bounine, by exploiting the patriotism of your exiled comrades—trading on their sacred loyalties.

BOUNINE. "Sacred loyalties." Rubbish, my dear Counsellor! It's the money you investors are after!

DRIVINITZ. That's a lie!

BOUNINE. The share our letter promised of the Tsar's millions.

DRIVINITZ. If the Princess Anastasia really existed, she could command not only our fortunes but our lives.

BOUNINE. I don't remember your rallying to the Tsar's support. You were out of Russia the first day of the revolution.

DRIVINITZ. That settles it! I am going straight to the police!

BOUNINE. *(Picking up* DRIVINITZ's *hat and throwing it at him)* Go! Go ahead!

(DRIVINITZ *starts to exit.*)

And a fine bunch of fools you will look when the Grand Duchess herself appears in court!

(DRIVINITZ *stops in door and turns.* PETROVIN *enters from up Right Center and closes door.*)

Yes. I shall have her brought in to court on a stretcher if necessary. She herself will insist on it. *(He sits in armchair.)*

DRIVINITZ. *(Crossing a step toward Center)* Very well, Prince Bounine, I will give you one last chance. You may have one week—one week in which to produce the Grand Duchess. If you fail to do so, we shall have a warrant issued for your arrest. Yours and your two companions. *(He exits.)*

BOUNINE. Sergei.

(SERGEI *appears in front doorway.*)

Show that gentleman out.

(SERGEI *exits, followed by* PETROVIN.)

CHERNOV. *(Crossing to* BOUNINE) One week! *(Crosses below table and around above to Left Center.)*

BOUNINE. *(Takes out cigarette and lights it.)* Makes you sweat, does it? It's easy to see, Chernov, you've never been shot at.

(CHERNOV *sits Right of table.)*
It's only at such a time the air has the same taste it had at our birth. Well, we're at one of those moments now— *(Rises.)* So take a deep breath. *(Crosses to Right Center door and opens it.)*

PETROVIN. *(Entering and shutting doors behind him)* One week!

BOUNINE. *(Calling off Right Center)* Varya! Bring the girl back up here.

VARYA. *(Off.)* Yes, Excellency.

(BOUNINE *closes door.)*

PETROVIN. *(Crossing down to above Left end of table)* But it's impossible. We can't even make her sufficiently convincing to say she deceived us.

BOUNINE. *(On platform at Center.)* We can make her convincing. We must.

CHERNOV. Not in one week.

BOUNINE. *(Crossing Left to above table, between* CHERNOV *and* PETROVIN) That may not be as bad as it sounds. At that first meeting she will be in bed with a nurse and a doctor in attendance.

CHERNOV. A doctor?

BOUNINE. I know a man who can safely be trusted. He'll tell them she is not to be pilloried with questions. For that occasion, her wounds will be sufficient evidence.

CHERNOV. And after that?

BOUNINE. Before the presentation to the shareholders I shall demand two months for convalescence. We'll say she's consumptive. That cough of hers will help.

PETROVIN. We'll have to see she doesn't lose it.

BOUNINE. *(Crossing below* CHERNOV *to crate down Right)* Plenty of cigarettes will take care of that.

CHERNOV. She hasn't agreed to do it yet.

BOUNINE. We'll make her agree.

(VARYA *opens Right Center door and pushes* ANNA *in.*)

Come in. Varya!

(VARYA *exits, closing door.*)

You see, you had no need to get so upset, Princess.

ANNA. I told you not to call me Princess.

BOUNINE. *(Crossing up to Right of armchair)* Why won't you admit it to us? You didn't mind the sisters knowing.

ANNA. *(On platform Center.)* The little nun? Yes, she believed it. Her eyes got big like saucers and in the evening she brought me some special things to eat—an orange and some grapes.

BOUNINE. That's the least she could do for a royal princess.

ANNA. But I could have told her other stories just as romantic. Of the time I went to the land of eternal ice with the three professors, the old one and two young ones—

BOUNINE. When was this?

ANNA. *(On steps.)* When? I don't remember. There was a great glacier and we had to chip the ice very carefully. Then the blocks were melted down by the professors. And in them were plants and strange creatures that lived on the earth ages and ages ago. We saw a butterfly that came alive and flew about in the sun. A butterfly that had lived for a million years and then died in one day.

BOUNINE. Romantic indeed!

ANNA. *(Crossing to above Right end of table, between* CHERNOV *and* PETROVIN) And in the other hospital where I stayed for so long they used to beg me to tell them my adventures. There was the blowing up of the train with the soldiers—we lay in the grass near the mouth of the tunnel and waited. But we were too close to where the mine was planted and when the train struck it, the pieces of metal fell all about us. The man beside me was killed and I was struck on the head and on my hands. That is how I got those scars, you see—

CHERNOV. I thought you didn't remember.

ANNA. *(Crossing down Left, below table)* I don't. Not always. Things seem to come and go—in the mists. *(Sites stool.)*

BOUNINE. I see you have been quite a reader, Fraulein. But I also see something else—you are an actress— *(He applauds.)* and an actress is what we want. *(Crosses to below table, Right of ANNA.)*

ANNA. You wish me to pretend the story I told the little nun is true?

BOUNINE. Exactly. You found out that it paid to tell it to her—you got an orange and some grapes. Tell it for us and you will get more—far, far more.

ANNA. The little nun was simple and trusting.

CHERNOV. *(Rising, to below Right end of table)* Yes, these people you are to meet will not be as easy to fool as your little nun. You will have to meet friends and members of the family.

ANNA. The family? They won't accept me. They will remember the princess as she was. They will say I'm lying.

BOUNINE. Even if they think you are lying they may still accept you.

ANNA. Why? Why should they?

BOUNINE. You might well be the key that would unlock doors for them—the doors of vaults. The Tsar deposited money abroad in an effort to provide for his children. Ten million pounds. A fortune that would now belong to his sole surviving heir.

ANNA. And would they take me in and pretend that they loved me because of money? Is that what they are like?

PETROVIN. *(Crossing to Left of BOUNINE)* Do you really think the Romanovs might endorse her?

BOUNINE. Some of them.

(CHERNOV *shakes head.*)

(BOUNINE *crosses to Center.)* Yes, if it were managed tactfully.

CHERNOV. *(Crossing to crate down Right)* Dreams! Crackbrained fancies!

PETROVIN. *(Crossing to Left of* BOUNINE *at Center)* Pay no attention. It's his gallstones talking. Tell me, who would carry the most weight?

BOUNINE. The most weight? No question about that—the Old Ikon.

PETROVIN. The Old Ikon?

BOUNINE. That is what we all used to call her. Maria Feodorovna—the Tsar's mother.

CHERNOV. *(Leaning against crate)* People say she went mad.

BOUNINE. She happens to be here in Berlin, visiting her grand-nephew, Paul.

PETROVIN. *(Crossing to* CHERNOV*)* That doesn't sound as if she were too crazy.

BOUNINE. Perhaps not too crazy, but definitely difficult. *(Crossing up Center)* I knew her well in the old days—a Tarter with a tongue like a whiplash.

PETROVIN. *(Crossing to behind armchair)* What about him?

BOUNINE. Him? Who?—who are you talking about?

PETROVIN. The Prince you say she is visiting, Prince Paul.

BOUNINE. *(Turning to* PETROVIN*)* I wonder? I wonder which way he would jump? *(Pointing to poster)* He was her future husband.

PETROVIN. Anastasia's?

BOUNINE. *(Crossing back to* PETROVIN, *Left of armchair)* There'd been no announcement of the betrothal, but everyone at Court took it as an accepted fact. The two had been playmates from childhood—second cousins.

CHERNOV. *(Crossing in to Right of* PETROVIN*)* Surely this Prince Paul would be the hardest to convince? He was in love with the girl—or was he?

BOUNINE. Royalty—who can tell? It was a great match for him. Aside from any question of rank, the Tsar was the richest man in the world. Yes—yes, the more I consider it—Paul is poor and pleasure-loving. That big fortune that's waiting in the banks would count a lot with him.

CHERNOV. But surely the only way he could get the money— My God, you don't think he'd be willing to marry that?

BOUNINE. It's a lot of money, remember.

ANNA. *(Rising)* No.

BOUNINE. *(Turning to* ANNA) What do you mean, "no"?

ANNA. *(Crossing below to Right end of table)* I want to go.

BOUNINE. Go where?

ANNA. *(Starts to front door.)* Anywhere. Back to the nuns—

PETROVIN. *(Crossing on platform to front door and drawing pistol)* Stop!

(CHERNOV *crosses to above armchair.*)

ANNA. *(Stops and turns to* BOUNINE.) I knew it—you brought me here to kill me. Kill me then. *(Crossing up steps to* PETROVIN) It doesn't matter.

(PETROVIN *points pistol at* ANNA.)

BOUNINE. *(Crossing up to Right of* ANNA) Put away that pistol, you fool.

PETROVIN. *(Pushing* ANNA *away from door)* You can't let her go now!

BOUNINE. She's not going anywhere. Anna— *(Restraining her)* We are not Bolsheviks who are trying to trap you.

ANNA. I can't do what you ask. It's impossible.

BOUNINE. *(Leading her to armchair and seating her.)*
 (CHERNOV *holds chair.* PETROVIN *to Right of chair.*)
It isn't, I tell you. All you have to do is to put yourself in our hands. There's enough likeness for you to carry it off. We will teach you the things that you'll need to know.

PETROVIN. *(Kneeling)* Don't you want to be a royal

princess and wear a coronet and have people kneel and kiss your hand?

ANNA. *(Cowering in the chair)* I think I must still be in the asylum with the woman who believes she is an angel, and the three who sit crouched and covered all day because they have not yet been born.

BOUNINE. Perhaps you are right. Here you are with the mad general, the mad painter, and the mad banker.

CHERNOV. *(Crossing below BOUNINE to Right edge of table)* Only the banker is not quite so mad as the others. You expect her to learn the names of half-a-dozen palaces, each with its servants and officials, the regiments who guarded them, tutors, titled friends, court procedure—quite a task for a woman with a bad memory.

BOUNINE. *(Following CHERNOV)* She will naturally make mistakes. But the lapse of time will excuse her—that, and her head wound.

CHERNOV. I doubt if she even knows how to behave among people of our class.

BOUNINE. Our class? Oh, I like that! You and the Grand Dukes, I suppose.

CHERNOV. At least I belong to that class parasitically.

BOUNINE. *(Stepping back)* A flea that has found its way under a coroneted shirt. That's a perfect description. —I must remember that.

(CHERNOV *sits on stool Left.)*

PETROVIN. You saw her hands. They're not those of a peasant.

BOUNINE. *(Takes chair Right of table, places it Left of armchair.)* We'll find out just how hard it will be to teach her.

ANNA. *(Rising)* Please, I'm so tired—I can't argue—please—let me go—

BOUNINE. *(Confronting her)* Where would you go? The canal?

ANNA. Perhaps—

BOUNINE. You have lived through a great deal. Why die now?

ANNA. Why live? There's only a flicker of difference.

BOUNINE. But the flicker is on the side of life. I saw that at the canal.

PETROVIN. You need food.

BOUNINE. And rest in a comfortable bed, warm clothes, shelter—

ANNA. *(Sits on armchair.)* Yes, I am an animal—like everyone else.

BOUNINE. *(Crossing behind ANNA)* So it is agreed? You put yourself in our hands?

ANNA. What if this princess—the real one—should suddenly appear?

BOUNINE. *(Crosses Right to crate and pours drink.)* You needn't worry. She's dead. I have first-hand information.

PETROVIN. She was murdered at Ekaterinburg with her entire family—a doctor, a governess, a valet and a cook—eleven in all.

BOUNINE. That is the official story. *(Pushes PETROVIN Right; gives ANNA drink.)*

(ANNA drinks.)

(BOUNINE takes glass, gives it to PETROVIN, who puts it on crate down Right.) But there's a rumor that you escaped with two brothers named Tchaikowsky who were members of your guard.

PETROVIN. No doubt she has heard that story.

ANNA. Some of it.

BOUNINE. You must know it in complete detail. *(He crosses to above ANNA to Left of armchair above.)* These two guards entered the shed where the murdered eleven awaited burial. They detected a movement and dragged you from the heap of the dead. Pay attention! *(Hits ANNA on the arm.)* This is the story you will have to tell. They hid you in a farm cart.

ANNA. In a farm cart.

BOUNINE. They trekked across Southern Siberia.

PETROVIN. You had jewels sewn in your skirt—they used them to get money.

BOUNINE. They moved on South, avoiding the towns and cities, making their way to—where was it, Piotr?

PETROVIN. Balta.

BOUNINE. Did you hear that?

ANNA. Balta.

BOUNINE. Good! And from there across the Rumanian border to Bucharest.

ANNA. Bucharest—yes—

BOUNINE. Bucharest is where we found you. We took you to Switzerland to a sanitarium—you will have to remember that too. *(Crossing above chair to Right of* ANNA*)* Now, who was it rescued you the night of the assassination?

ANNA. Two brothers named Tchaikowsky.

BOUNINE. And they took you across the Rumanian border at what place?

ANNA. Balta. And from there to Bucharest where you found me.

BOUNINE. *(Crossing to Right of table)* There! What have you to say to that, my dear high-class flea?

CHERNOV. This is nothing. There are endless details, names, relationships—

BOUNINE. It will mean work, certainly—but she has shown us that she can learn.

PETROVIN. This might be a good time to introduce her to her family.

BOUNINE. Yes, bring one of those albums of photographs. *(Crosses and sits Left of* ANNA.*)*

*(*PETROVIN *crosses to up Right crate for album.* CHERNOV *picks up album from table.)*

ANNA. The family that you said I will have to meet. Who are they?

BOUNINE. The most important are your second cousin once removed, Prince Paul—known also by his German title, Heraldeberg—and your grandmother, the Dowager Empress, Maria Feodorovna.

ANNA. My grandmother—will I meet her?

BOUNINE. If we are lucky. That will be, I admit, your most trying experience.

(Beckons to CHERNOV, who brings album.)

But it will not take place until after weeks of lessons.

PETROVIN. *(Crosses down to BOUNINE with album and takeks album which CHERNOV has brought to crate up Right.)* This is the best one.

(CHERNOV crosses Left and leans against table.)

BOUNINE. You must remember that you loved your family. You more than any of the other children.

ANNA. I loved my family—

BOUNINE. And so you should. From your ancestors you derive their grandeur, from the murdered dead their tragic dignity, and from the survivors their distinction. Look—here is the first one—your mother, Queen Alexandra. Why do you close your eyes? Is your eyesight weak?

ANNA. No. Go on.

BOUNINE. The Grand Duke Sergius, your Uncle Serge. I once heard him say that the way to recognize a lady was by her laugh. He was an authority on laughter and boasted that even when drunk or in the pitch dark he could recognize his wife's laugh and so could avoid meeting her. And this is your Uncle Michael, who used to dance for the Court as beautifully as one of Diaghileff's stars—

CHERNOV. You won't meet either of them. They were shot by a Bolshevik firing squad.

BOUNINE. And this is one of the whole family on the deck of your father's yacht.

ANNA. *The Standart.*

(PETROVIN and CHERNOV cross in a step.)

BOUNINE. You know that, do you?

ANNA. The name is on the life preserver, there by her side.

BOUNINE. Ah, so it is.

(PETROVIN *returns up Right; leans on crate.* CHERNOV *crosses and sits in chair above table.*)

And here's one of you, standing on the bridge of what we used to call the Chinese Island.

ANNA. She's waving to someone.

BOUNINE. *(Turning pages)* Uncles and aunts—there's quite a series of them. Say their names after me— The Grand Duchess Marie Pavlovna—Aunt Miechen.

ANNA. Aunt Miechen.

BOUNINE. The Duchess of Cumberland—Aunt Thyra.

ANNA. Aunt Thyra.

BOUNINE. The King of Norway—Uncle Hans.

ANNA. Uncle Hans.

BOUNINE. The Queen of Norway—Aunt Swan.

ANNA. Aunt Swan.

BOUNINE. The old King of England—Uncle Bertie.

ANNA. Uncel Bertie. *(She laughs.)*

CHERNOV. And how much of all that can she repeat?

BOUNINE. We'll go over the list every day. Now look —we'll close the book on this one—you in uniform as Colonel of the Kaspiski Regiment.

PETROVIN. *(Crossing down to Right of* ANNA) Blue skirt, red dolman, kolpak of black fur.

ANNA. Dolman?

BOUNINE. The shoulder cape. You are on the way to review your regiment.

PETROVIN. *(Pulling* ANNA *to below steps below door up Left Center)* Let us re-enact it. Perhaps that will make her see it.

BOUNINE. *(Rises, moves his chair to down Right, puts album on crate.)* Good, Piotr! Good!

PETROVIN. Go up those steps. They are the steps of the Winter Palace—your father's palace.

CHERNOV. Childish.

PETROVIN. *(Backing to below Right Center door on platform)* Now turn and face us.

BOUNINE. *(Crosses above armchair to platform.)* Try to picture it. The long line of the Imperial Guard—your father, the Emperor, in uniform, at their head. Behind you, on a balcony, are the white specks that are your mother, your sisters, and your brother Alexis. Grouped below are the palace guards and servants, the Negroes with their feathered turbans. The massed bands strike up. *(Singing)* God protect the Tsar!

> *(He starts to sing the Russian anthem: "Boje Tsarya khranyi Silni derjavni," etc., with* PETROVIN *stamping to keep time. There is a momentary pause.* ANNA *grasps skirt as if it were a riding habit; then erect, head up, quite altered in her carriage, she comes down the steps as though walking to slow music.)*

Splendid! I believe she can do it!

PETROVIN. Yes!

BOUNINE. *(Crossing down Center, off platform)* And now let me introduce you to the members of your household. Boris Chernov. Formerly of St. Petersburg. Banker.

(CHERNOV *nods.)*

PETROVIN. *(Crossing to below and Right of armchair, bowing)* Piotr Constantinovitch Petrovin. Artist. Formerly of the scenic department, Russian Imperial Opera.

BOUNINE. Prince Arcade Arcadievitch Bounine, General of the Don Cossacks, former Aide-de-Camp attached to the person of His Imperial Majesty Nicholas the Second, Tsar of all the Russias.

ANNA. *(With raised head and in an imperious tone.)* And I? I am Her Imperial Highness, Princess Anastasia Nicholaevna.

(There is a beat of silence. Then she bursts into a discordant laugh which sends her into a fit of coughing.)

CURTAIN

ACT TWO

*The set is now brilliantly lit. On the Right wall are hung
all sorts of Russian ikons and a picture of the Tsarevitch. In the up Right corner is a large ornate tile
stove. On the back wall are more ikons. "Anna's"
door, up Left Center, is hung with beautiful draperies
the same scheme being carried out in the window
down Left. Down stage of the front door in the Left
wall is an ikon with a small ikon light beneath it—
lighted. Down Right is a large ornate cabinet with
small footstool underneath. On the cabinet is a
bronze horse, decanters, bottles of brandy and vodka,
glasses, cigarettes, matches and ash tray. Left of
cabinet against the bottom step is a straight gold
chair. Right Center is a gold settee with cushions.
Left of settee is a round gold table with a photograph
album, ash tray, cigarettes, matches and a picture
of the Russian royal family in an ornate frame sur-
mounted with the Russian eagles. Against the wall
up Center between the doors is a table with ash
tray, matches and a vase of blue flowers. Down Left
is a square gold table with two gold armchairs on
either side. On the table are ash tray, matches, two
table-sized ikons, a candelabra, a silver salt and pep-
per set. Sunlight comes through the big double window.*

It is about 3 P.M.

(SERGEI *enters smoking a cigarette and carrying two ash
trays. Places one on table Left of settee and crosses
down Right to put the second on the cabinet. He
looks around and helps himself to a drink of vodka.*)

36

VARYA. *(Enters from up Left Center—sees* SERGEI *and assumes a deep voice.)* Sergei!

SERGEI. *(Putting the glass down quickly and turning)* Oh, it's you.

(BOTH *laugh.)*

Want some?

VARYA. His Excellency is out?

SERGEI. All afternoon. Where's the girl?

VARYA. *(Crossing down Left, arranging armchair above table)* Her Imperial Highness is having a bit of a rest. She hasn't done so well today.

SERGEI. You mean the old Chamberlain?

VARYA. *(Crossing to Left of table Right Center)* He wouldn't accept her.

SERGEI. No, but just as I was leading him out he turned round and called back, "Tell me, who are you?"

VARYA. What did she do?

SERGEI. Stared steadily at him and gave him no answer.

VARYA. *(Helps herself to a handful of cigarettes from box on table.)* She's clever all right.

(PETROVIN *enters from up Right Center with glass of tea.* VARYA *starts for up Left Center door, hiding cigarettes.)*

PETROVIN. What are you doing going around without your coat.

SERGEI. I didn't want to get it dirty.

(PETROVIN *intercepts* VARYA *and holds out his hand. She gives him the cigarettes.)*

VARYA. He fancies himself in that royal livery. (VARYA *exits Left Center, closing curtains.)*

PETROVIN. You know we've got to keep up appearances. There are still some people out there.

SERGEI. *(Picking up uniform coat from chair Right)* People of no importance.

PETROVIN. *(Crossing down Center)* How many?

SERGEI. *(Putting on coat)* Three. The dressmaker had to go.

PETROVIN. Sonya Rykoff?

SERGEI. Yes, that is the one. She'll be back tomorrow.

PETROVIN. Tell these people Her Highness will see them in a little while.

SERGEI. *(Crosses below settee and exits front door.)* Yes sir.

PETROVIN. *(Sits on settee with tea.)* And don't forget to say Her Highness.

CHERNOV. *(Enters from up Right Center from upstairs, closes door.)* Well, Piotr, how's it going?

PETROVIN. Ups and downs. The peasants, most of them, accept her without question.

CHERNOV. *(Crossing down Left Center)* The illiterates, of course. They're always the loyal ones. It was Alexander the Second with those damned schools of his that made the Russian revolution. *(He winces audibly.)*

PETROVIN. What's the matter? Your gallstones?

CHERNOV. It's a question of tension. They haven't been quiet since the day of that bedside visit of Drivinitz and his pack of sceptics. *(He crosses Left to chair upstage of table Left.)*

PETROVIN. They were not quqite so sceptical after seeing her wounds.

CHERNOV. No, but next time she meets them there won't be a doctor to forbid her talking.

(SERGEI *opens doors up Left, admitting* BOUNINE, *who gives coat to* SERGEI, *who closes doors and exits Right Center.)*

BOUNINE. Good afternoon, gentlemen.

PETROVIN. *(Rises, puts tea on cabinet down Right.)* Good afternoon, Excellency.

BUONINE. *(On platform.)* I have news. We are about to receive a distinguished visitor.

PETROVIN. Oh?

BOUNINE. *(Crossing down Center)* Maria Feodorovna, the Old Ikon herself.

(PETROVIN *crosses to Right of* BOUNINE *at Center.* CHERNOV *crosses to Left of* BOUNINE.)

(Straightening CHERNOV'S *tie)* It's official. The Prince sent for me to ask if Her Highness was now well enough for us to bring to Haraldeberg to meet the Empress. I thought we weren't ready for that—not yet—so I said "no." *(Turning to* PETROVIN *and surveying him.)*

PETROVIN. Quite right, but—

BOUNINE. The Prince said, "in that case Her Mejesty will visit Her Highness here under my escort." Of course there was nothing I could reply to that except that I was sure Her Highness would be overjoyed. *(Crosses to settee and sits.)*

(SERGEI *enters Right Center with silver tray.)*

CHERNOV. Were those his exact words? Did he actually say "Her Highness"?

(VARYA *enters Right Center with tea. Puts it on cabinet down Right and clears* PETROVIN'S *tea.)*

BOUNINE. *(Buffing his nails)* He did indeed. No talk of "the unknown woman," or "the alleged daughter of the Tsar"—the sort of phrases he used before he met her.

PETROVIN. It sounds as if she'd convinced him.

BOUNINE. I think she has.

(VARYA *exits Right Center with tea.)*

PETROVIN. I don't wonder. She's amazing. What she's managed to learn in one month—

CHERNOV. *(Crossing to table Left)* Five weeks.

BOUNINE. *(Combing beard)* Her ability at picking out and memorizing petty detail is certainly extraordinary.

PETROVIN. Yes, if that is what it is.

(CHERNOV *sits in chair above table Left.*)

BOUNINE. What on earth do you mean?

PETROVIN. Well, it seems to me at times that it passes the extraordinary and becomes the uncanny.

(SERGEI *takes tray to cabinet—brings tea to* BOUNINE. *Picks up tray again and stands waiting Right of settee.*)

CHERNOV. Rubbish! She's made mistakes—plenty of them—when we've been going over the books of data.

PETROVIN. *(Crossing to* CHERNOV) Oh yes, the name of some functionary, or whether some event took place at Tsarskoie or the Winter Palace—the sort of mistakes we would all make about things that happened ten or twelve years ago.

BOUNINE. Piotr— You surely aren't suggesting—?

PETROVIN. *(Crossing back to Center)* Are you sure Anastasia was killed?

BOUNINE. Of course she was killed. I had the whole story from Yourovski's head bodyguard before we strung him up. To be sure Anastasia fainted when Yourovski shot her father and so the first volley of the firing squad didn't kill her. She woke up to find ten corpses lying all about her. If she hadn't screamed she might have stood a chance.

CHERNOV. The bodies were tossed down a deserted mine shaft. You don't suppose Yourovski didn't count them, do you?

PETROVIN. All the same the tale of her escape has also been insisted on by people who claimed to have first-hand information.

(BOUNINE *puts tea on tray and dismisses* SERGEI. *He exits Right Center.*)

BOUNINE. Russian peasants. You know their love of the miraculous.

PETROVIN. It's a choice of miracles it seems to me.

CHERNOV. With all this perfection you see in her I will remind you of one glaring failure. There must be an interpreter present if she talks to a witness who can only speak Russian.

PETROVIN. Yes, yes, that's true.

BOUNINE. *(Taking album from table Left of settee)* All that won't matter if only the Old Ikon accepts her. Everything depends on that.

PETROVIN. What time will they be here?

BOUNINE. About four.

PETROVIN. Less than an hour. *(Crossing to front door)* Perhaps I'd better send away the remaining witnesses and we'll give her a last minute drilling on one of the albums.

BOUNINE. No! It would only confuse her mind and make her nervous. No, we'll have to trust to her instinct. *(Looking at photo in album)* Of course it's ten years since I've seen the Empress. It's not likely her own memory is what it was. She's nearly eighty, remember.

SERGEI. *(Knocks and enters front door.)* Pardon, Excellency, there is a phone call from a newspaper.

BOUNINE. Which one?

SERGEI. *Die Nachtausgabe. (He exits.)*

PETROVIN. *(Starting out)* They called before asking for an interview.

BOUNINE. *(Rising)* Stay here! You'd better talk to them, Chernov.

PETROVIN. *(Stopping at upstage side of doors)* Why do you say that?

BOUNINE. *(Crossing up Center)* Be careful, make her health the excuse. Don't annoy them.

(CHERNOV *exits front door.)*

You're not to be trusted with newspaper people. Giving out her photograph for publication was the act of an idiot. *(Crossing Right on platform.)*

PETROVIN. You said you wanted publicity.

VARYA. *(Entering Left Center)* Pardon, Excellency, Her Highness is ready to receive the witnesses.

(BOUNINE *gestures to* PETROVIN.)

PETROVIN. *(Opens front door and calls off.)* Sergei!

BOUNINE. Who are they?

PETROVIN. *(Crossing Right on platform to* BOUNINE) A sleigh-driver, a shabby-looking doctor and some sort of charwoman—nobody who matters.

(SERGEI *enters front door.)*

BOUNINE. Their names may help to swell the list of supporters. You explained why Her Highness prefers to conduct these interviews in German?

(PETROVIN *gestures to* SERGEI.)

SERGEI. Yes, Excellency, I told them it was so that the records of what was said could be read by her legal advisers.

BOUNINE. Good.

PETROVIN. One at a time, Sergei, the woman first.

SERGEI. The old man and the woman are friends. They asked if they may come together.

PETROVIN. Very well.

(SERGEI *exits front door.)*

BOUNINE. *(To* VARYA.) Tell Her Highness we are ready.

(VARYA *exits Left Center.* BOUNINE *crosses to Left of stove.)*

SERGEI. *(Enters.)* Come—this way.

(CHARWOMAN *and* SLEIGH DRIVER *enter and cross down Left Center.* CHARWOMAN *crosess herself at the ikon.* SERGEI *closes door and stands in doorway.)*

PETROVIN. *(Crossing down to them)* Now, my good people, Her Royal Highness is about to receive you. You are to talk to her and examine her attentively. After the audience you will be taken to the Chief Secretary who will register your opinion in writing and obtain your signature. *(He crosses up Center on platform and bows.)*

(Curtains Left Center are opened by VARYA. *She crosses doorway and bows.)*

SERGEI. Her Imperial Highness Anastasia Nicolaevna

(SERGEI *bows.* TWO OLD PEOPLE *drop to their knees.* ANNA *enters to Left Center.)*

SLEIGH DRIVER. *(Reaching out for* ANNA'S *hand and kissing it)* Yes, it is you, Little Mother. I know you as my dog knows me. You were like four flowers, you and your sisters, and for each of you there was a different scent.

ANNA. Dear Wasseievitch! Do you remember that Christmas at Gatchina when I had sprained my ankle on the ice and you had to carry me to and from your sleigh in your arms?

SLEIGH DRIVER. Yes, it is your voice. I would know it anywhere.

ANNA. I remember how you used to kiss each of your horses good morning. And I remember the big blue silk net that was spread over their backs to keep the snow they kicked up from falling on the people who rode in the sleigh.

SLEIGH DRIVER. Yes, yes, Little Mother; I see you have not forgotten those old days.

ANNA. *(Turning to table Left of settee)* My sister Olga took a photograph of us, you and me. I have it in an album. Would you like to see it?

SLEIGH DRIVER. I am blind, Gracious One.

ANNA. I didn't know.

SLEIGH DRIVER. A double cataract. But I do not mind. It was a beautiful world that I saw in those old days. I like to pretend I am still living in it.

CHARWOMAN. You would be glad of your eyes today. Our princess is beautiful.

ANNA. *(Raising him to his feet)* You have knelt to me long enough, Wassaievitch. It was not like that at Gatchina. Then we threw snowballs at each other—only I knew you always threw them so that they should not hit me.

(PETROVIN *crosses Right and sits in chair above cabinet.)*

SLEIGH DRIVER. You loved the snow. I called you "Snow Princess' and you said you liked the name.

(BOUNINE *crosses down Right of settee.)*

PETROVIN. I'm really enjoying myself.
ANNA. Place chairs for my visitors.

(SERGEI *crosses to down Left chair and* VARYA *to chair above table.)*

BOUNINE. *(Crossing to front of settee)* I must inform Your Highness that other visitors are coming— Prince Paul and the Empress Mother.
ANNA. *She* is coming here?
BOUNINE. Yes.
ANNA. I don't know if I will be able to face her.
BOUNINE. Why not?
ANNA. I am not sure that I am well enough. Must it be today?
BOUNINE. Yes, it must. I will send these peasants away. *(Crosses to* PEASANTS.) Then you can lie down and rest.

(VARYA *and* SERGEI *start to take* PEASANTS *out.)*

ANNA. No! They have been waiting a long time. Bring the chairs.

(SERGEI *brings down Left chair to Left Center.* VARYA *brings chair above table to Center.* BOUNINE *glares at* ANNA, *moves Center chair slightly more Left Center and crosses up Right on platform.* SERGEI *crosses to above window,* VARYA *to Left of front door.)*

ANNA. *(Sitting on settee)* Sit here. What is your name?

(CHARWOMAN *helps* SLEIGH DRIVER *into Left chair and sits in Right chair.)*

CHARWOMAN. Annouchka, Highness.

ANNA. And have you come here all the way from Russia, Annouchka?

CHARWOMAN. No, Highness, I have lived here in the Russian colony since 1921.

ANNA. You know me, do you, Annouchka?

CHARWOMAN. Of course I know you, Little Mother.

ANNA. Where was it that I met you? In Peterhof, Lavadia or was it in Spala during the war?

CHARWOMAN. At Ekaterinburg, Little Mother.

ANNA. You saw me there? But nobody was allowed in the town except the soldiers.

CHARWOMAN. I lived there. And so they sent me into the accursed house with the two wooden fences about, with the closed windows and the darkened panes. The soldiers said to me "You are to wash the floor boards," so I went in.

ANNA. And you saw me there?

CHARWOMAN. *(Rises.)* Sitting in a half-dark room all alone. I had my pail, my cloths, my brushes. Yourovski, that assassin, gave me a push and said "hurry." I fell on my knees on the threshold of the room as one does in church. That vile one thought it was in order to scrub the floor but you knew it was for you that I knelt.

ANNA. For me——?

CHARWOMAN. You smiled and gave me a good wish, and then you forgot I was there. Your thoughts were in the clouds flying like wounded birds.

ANNA. I remember. I do remember. I remember the

swish of your cloth as you wiped the floors reminded me of the frou-frou of the women's trains as they walked about the polished floors of the Winter Palace. *(She rises, crossing Left of* CHARWOMAN.*)* And I thought of the wonderful balls that were given there. That great staircase—and on every step a huntsman in green, his gloved hand on a gilt cutlass.

CHARWOMAN. One of the soldiers had traced on the floor a sketch of Rasputin all naked. I washed it out and as I did so, the sun must have come out, for a little beam came through the shutters and there on the floor was your shadow. I stooped and kissed it. And afterwards came that dreadful day when the shots were heard, and the sun darkened so that a July evening seemed like the blackest hour in winter.

(ANNA *falls to her knees.* CHARWOMAN *holds* ANNA *in her arms. General movement from the* CONSPIRATORS.*)*

But even then, at that time, it was whispered that there was one who was *not* dead. And as the months passed and we gathered round our stoves, the story was told of the Princess who was carried away in the night, in her bloodstained dress, all heavy with the diamonds and pearls sewn together and the tale of him who had exchanged for ten big diamonds the droshka and the horses—

BOUNINE. *(Crossing from Right, below settee, lifts* ANNA *to her feet and crosses above Right end of settee.)*

(ANNA *sits on settee.)*

Enough! Her Highness must close the audience.

(SERGEI *leads* SLEIGH DRIVER *to front door.* VARYA *pulls* CHARWOMAN *half way up steps Center.)*

You were brought here to attest that this is indeed Anastasia Nicolaevna. You both agree?

CHARWOMAN. In Ekaterinburg there is a deep forest of pine trees and in it in the night shadows are seen moving dressed in silver and lovely as the moon. Four daughters—they say four—but I know there can only be three.

SLEIGH DRIVER. *(As* SERGEI *leads him out)* Bless Your Highness.

CHARWOMAN. *(As* VARYA *drags her out)* Matushka, matushka, nasha, my syerotih bez tsibyah, vyerniss knam. (Little Mother, Little Mother of ours, we are orphans without you, return to us.)

ANNA. Goodbye, Annouchka, Annouchka of Ekaterinburg.

PETROVIN. *(Crosses to front door, watching them out, and closes door.)* Thank heaven! I'm dying for a cigarette. *(Crosses down Center, taking cigarette from table, and lights match.)*

ANNA. *(Crossing to* PETROVIN, *takes cigarette from him and throws it to floor.)* How dare you? How dare you light a cigarette in my presence without my permission?

PETROVIN. I beg your Highness' pardon. If you'll excuse me I'll— Strange! *(He exits front door.)*

BOUNINE. Good! Most effective. And does that mean that your illusion has returned? Or is it self-hypnotism?

ANNA. *(Sitting settee)* May I have a cigarette please.

BOUNINE. *(Puts cigarette in* ANNA's *mouth and lights it.)* Have I Your Highness' permission— *(He lights own cigarette.)* Anyhow you have managed to capture just the right tone. *(Crosses above to Right of settee.)* If you are as good with the old Empress as you were with those two servants the prize is in sight. The Prince will be here too. I am sure he is only waiting for the Empress' acknowledgment to remind you that he was your girlhood fiancé.

ANNA. And am I to marry him?

BOUNINE. It may sound overly ambitious.

ANNA. And am I to have children brought into the world at your command? And must they me his? Or will you allow me the liberty of my famous ancestress and let me choose my Orloffs or my Potemkins?

BOUNINE. Don't speak to me in that mocking tone or you will get your face slapped. Your success with these Muzhiks has gone to your head. If you are clever it is with my cleverness. *(Sits Right arm of settee.)* The Prince is a romantic sentimentalist. He will persuade himself he is in love with you—if that is at all important.

ANNA. "If that is at all important"? Why should it be? Can a poor outcast expect everything?

BOUNINE. Outcast certainly. But I've come to realize something that was not altogether evident at our first meeting. You are well educated, refined—who are you? From what family do you come?

ANNA. My father was a toymaker, my mother his assistant who painted the faces of his dolls. Could you ask a better ancestry for a puppet?

SERGEI. *(Entering front door)* Pardon, Excellency. What of the last witness?

BOUNINE. *(Rising)* Who is it?

SERGEI. The doctor. He's been waiting a long time.

SERENSKY. *(Entering, followed by* CHERNOV*)* I am sure the Princess will see me.

SERGEI. *(Restraining him)* You can't come in here.

SERENSKY. She saw the others.

ANNA. *(Rises and crosses Right to cabinet—puts out cigarette.)* Michael!

BOUNINE. Let him come in. *(Crosses Center.)* Her Highness can grant you only a brief interview. She is expecting some important visitors, and so is preoccupied.

SERENSKY. Yes, so I see.

(SERGEI *exits front door.*)

BOUNINE. What is your name?

SERENSKY. Michael Serensky. I am a doctor.

CHERNOV. *(Left of* SERENSKY.*)* Where was it you met Her Highness?

SERENSKY. In the hospital.

BOUNINE. One that she visited with her mother during the war?

SERENSKY. No. One in which we were both patients.

CHERNOV. Where was this?

SERENSKY. In Bucharest.

(BOUNINE *crosses to* CHERNOV *at front door.*)
We used to sit in the big sun room together and talk. *(He crosses down Center.)* Her head had been hurt in a fac-

tory explosion. With all those bandages it was impossible to tell whether she was pretty or ugly. But I liked her voice. We became great friends. (*Sits Center.*)

CHERNOV. He's here to make trouble.

BOUNINE. (*Crosses down Left of* SERENSKY.). Yes, so I begin to realize. You're a Bolshevik agent!

CHERNOV. (*Crosses to Right of* SERENSKY.) They've sent you to upset Her Highness' claim.

SERENSKY. You know she is not Her Highness as well as I do.

BOUNINE. Keep your eyes on me, you Bolshevik dog. I am talking to you.

SERENSKY. I am not a Bolshevik, and I am not their emissary.

CHERNOV. Who gave you a passport to come here? Who gave you the money?

SERENSKY. I have money of my own. Anya helped me in my laboratory. She is clever and except for this delusion about her family, quite sane.

CHERNOV. Is this true what this man is saying? Do you know him?

SERENSKY. (*Rising and crossing Right Center*) Of course she does. Aren't you going to speak to me, Anya? It's more than a year since we last saw each other, since you ran away.

BOUNINE. (*Crosses up Left on platform, gestures for* SERGEI, *who appears in front door and beckons to* CHERNOV, *who crosses up to him.*) Never mind that. Get out of here.

ANNA. No! Let him talk if he wants to. But it will do no good.

(CHERNOV *crosses up to* BOUNINE.)

SERENSKY. I have been lonely since you left, Anya. `

ANNA. I came here for a purpose, Michael. But it is no use to tell you.

SERENSKY. (*Crossing to* ANNA) Have you forgotten that evening in the field of sunflowers when you hid and

I caught you—and you lay with your head on one of the broken sunflowers like a pillow—and the moon shone in your face?

(ANNA *turns away.*)

I see—a royal gesture of dismissal. *(Turning away from her and crossing Center.)*

ANNA. You shouldn't be here, Michael. I don't need you.

SERENSKY. *(Circling to above settee)* I think you do. You're in dangerous hands.

BOUNINE. *(On steps Left Center.)* What's that?

SERENSKY. You should be ashamed, Prince Bounine. You think you can bring a dream to life and set it to work for you like a genii out of a bottle.

BOUNINE. *(Puts cigarette out at up Center table.)* That's enough.

SERENSKY. Stir up your memory, Anya. You remember how we worked together—the way you helped me with the slides and the tissues. Your hands were more skillful than mine—you were helping to save lives.

BOUNINE. *(Crosses down Right between* ANNA *and* SERENSKY.)

(CHERNOV *crosses Center on platform.*)

Didn't you hear me? Enough, I said. I'll have my servant kick you down the steps.

(SERGEI *crosses Center on platform.*)

SERENSKY. Be careful. I have her police papers, papers that establish her identity as Anya Bronin.

BOUNINE. Let me see them.

SERENSKY. Ah no, I haven't them on me, my dear Prince. I am not quite as trusting as that.

CHERNOV. Police papers are nothing. They are being forged every day. *(Crosses to front doorway Left Center and waits, watching.)*

BOUNINE. *(Crosses below settee to Right of table down Left.)* Sergei!

(SERGEI *crosses to Right of* SERENSKY *and above.*)

SERENSKY. *(Crossing up Center on platform)* You need summon no reinforcements. I am going.

BOUNINE. And don't come back or you will be sorry.

SERENSKY. I was for one year in the hands of the GPU. They wrecked my health and my reason for a time. After that what any man can do to me is nothing. Goodbye, Anya. If you should want me I'm at a small hotel called the Templehof. *(He exits, followed by* SERGEI.)

CHERNOV. Is that true? Has he got your police papers? If so, I'd better be sure Sergei doesn't manhandle him. *(He exits.)*

BOUNINE. *(Closes doors. Crossing down Center.)* So! Now it's Anya! It seems revolutions make strange bedfellows. Only it wasn't a bed—a field of sunflowers, the raw earth, like animals.

ANNA. You sound shocked. Don't tell me your moral sense is offended?

BOUNINE. You who pretend to be so aloof and so indifferent.

ANNA. Why are you so concerned?

BOUNINE. *(Crossing to* ANNA) Were you this cripple's mistress?

ANNA. And if I was, is that any business of yours?

BOUNINE. So that's your answer. Well, at least your lover has cleared the air for us. Now we know where we stand.

ANNA. Is that a warning that I had better keep my bedroom door locked?

BOUNINE. You may take it as a suggestion that you leave it open.

ANNA. You flatter yourself, Prince Bounine. I have no doubt there are some women who find you quite devastating. I happen not to be one of them. *(Starts to Left, above* BOUNINE.)

BOUNINE. *(Holding her by the arm)* A challenge? We will see. It might be amusing to give you some lessons in refined love making.

ANNA. Is this quite the moment? The Empress is coming, remember. The success or failure of your enterprise will be in my hands.

BOUNINE. *(Releasing her)* It can wait.

(ANNA *crosses Center above settee on steps.)*
And now you'd better concentrate on the questions you are to answer. *(He sits settee.)* Remember that though you were born in Peterhoff most of your childhood memories would be of Livadia, the palace on the Black Sea. If she mentions the money pretend you have no interest in it—you're not listening!—And most important the children called her "Grandmamma"—as it's pronounced in French.

ANNA. Grandmamma—yes—

PETROVIN. *(Entering front door an dcrossing down Left Center)* Sergei tells me that this doctor fellow is trying to upset things.

BOUNINE. *(Rises; crosses Right to cabinet.)* He saw the photograph that you so stupidly gave to the press and came straight to Berlin, armed with her police papers.

PETROVIN. Police papers? It's true then—he knows you?—knows who you are?

ANNA. Doctor Serensky? Oh yes, for a long time he was my doctor and afterwards, we were friends. He has explained to Prince Bounine about the crazy fancies that come to me at times. You see, my head was injured in a factory explosion. *(She exits up Left Center.)*

PETROVIN. Does she mean that? Is it the truth?

BOUNINE. The truth about her? How is anyone to know?

SERGEI. *(Entering front door)* Her Majesty's car is here.

BOUNINE. *(Arranges cushions and photo on table.)* Quick, Piotr, go and tell Anna she must hurry.

PETROVIN. *(Replacing the chairs)* Does she know what she is to wear?

BOUNINE. Yes, that is all arranged. *(Crosses Right to above table.)*

(PETROVIN *exits Left Center.)*

SERGEI. *(Entering)* Her Imperial Majesty.

EMPRESS. *(Enters, followed by* LIVENBAUM *and* CHER-NOV.) The royal livery? They're wasting no time, are they?

(CHERNOV *nods to* SERGEI, *who exits front door.)*
And Arcade Arcadievitch. I thought you were dead. Don't they shoot traitors nowadays?

BOUNINE. Let Your Majesty be reassured. The tradition has been observed. I was sentenced to be shot twice.

EMPRESS. By whom? The Whites or the Reds?

BOUNINE. By both.

EMPRESS. And you are still here? But then, I remember —you were always a man who, when you came to a parting of the ways, took both ways.

BOUNINE. It seems to me that our cause has had enough martyrs, Your Majesty. *(Crosses Right, below settee, and gestures for* EMPRESS *to sit.)* What it has chiefly lacked are men with practical minds who know how to gauge an opportunity and seize it when it appears.

EMPRESS. As you are doing here. The effrontery of using the name of Romanov to create a business, with share and salaried officers, and a promise of handsome dividends. My compliments, Bounine. You are a scoundrel on the grand scale.

(CHERNOV *exits; closes front doors.)*

LIVENBAUM. Oh, Your Majesty!

EMPRESS. Keep quiet.

(EMPRESS *crosses down Right Center to below settee;* LIVENBAUM *to above Left end of settee.)*

BOUNINE. *(Placing footstool for* EMPRESS) Either a scoundrel, Your Majesty, or possibly a loyal servitor of a Princess too long denied her rightful heritage. *(Backs to down Right of settee.)*

EMPRESS. *(Pushing stool under settee with umbrella and sitting)* You have certainly come some distance since those days when you were aide-de-camp to my elder son, gambling to the small hours with the Grand Dukes and winning ten thousand roubles a night—so I was told, with suspicious regularity.

BOUNINE. It is not necessary to cheat opponents who pour their brandy out in goblets.

EMPRESS. I remember one of your mistresses from the Marinskaia Theatre—you went in for actresses even in those days. She was French, if I remember rightly, and had eyes like a letter of mourning. She created a scandal in your rooms and my husband called you to account.

BOUNINE. Alas, Your Majesty! The lady acted when off the stage and behaven when on it.—An unfortunate reversal.

EMPRESS. She conveniently disappeared so that you were free to tell whatever story you liked. In those days you made women disappear and now you make them appear—quite a talented magician.

BOUNINE. The Grand Duchess Anastasia asked Your Majesty to grant her an interview at which you might judge, better than anyone living, the truth of her claim. She had relied, as had we, on your coming with an open mind.

EMPRESS. My dear Bounine, I have already been shown two Tatianas, an Alexis, and a Marie. I am a little weary of these spectral Romanovs. But I'm not here to spoil your little game—though I'm not here to help it either. I've come, if you must know, because my nephew has plagued me into it.

BOUNINE. I am grateful to His Highness.

EMPRESS. But I warn you, Bounine, don't try my patience too far. I have lost everything that I have ever loved—my husband, both my sons, my five grandchildren, my home, my position, my country—I have nothing left but my memories. Don't lay your hands on those—they are sacred. Now you may go.

BOUNINE. *(Bowing)* Thank you, Your Majesty. *(He crosses Center, then up Center and stops.)*

EMPRESS. I see you hesitate. Perhaps you are afraid to let your artist perform without a prompter.

BOUNINE. Not at all. I will go and tell Her Highness you are ready to receive her. *(Crosses to Left Center door—turns back.)* I think Your Majesty is about to meet with some surprises. *(He exits.)*

(LIVENBAUM *looks out door after him.*)

EMPRESS. A poisonous insect!

LIVENBAUM. *(Crosses down Right of settee.)* But he's attractive!—So masterful and ruthless. A blow or a kiss, or perhaps both.

EMPRESS. I find your voluptuous fancies quite disgusting. To a woman of your age sex should mean nothing but gender.

LIVENBAUM. Did he really murder the lady with the spaniel's eyes?

EMPRESS. I didn't say he murdered her—she just disappepared—

PAUL. *(Off.)* Where? In here?

LIVENBAUM. Ah—Prince Paul—

PAUL. *(Entering, crosses to Left of EMPRESS.)* You're here before me. I'm so sorry. I had to borrow a car. It's a nuisance not having one of your own.

EMPRESS. It's a pity your ancestors hadn't foreseen a time in which royalty might have to work for a living.

PAUL. *(Crosses Center, puts hat and gloves on table and coat on chair.)* Hasn't anyone received you?

EMPRESS. Oh, yes, Bounine was here. It's when I meet a man like that that I understand why the revolution happened.

PAUL. You hate him for having been Kerensky's satellite. *(Crosses down Left Center.)* There are plenty who made that mistake. The Bounine of 1917 and Bounine today are two different men.

EMPRESS. You think people change? How naive you are! My husband used to say "if you want to reform a man start with his grandfather."

PAUL. *(Sitting Left of* EMPRESS *on settee)* Well, any-way, don't quarrel with the dinner because you don't like the cook.

(LIVENBAUM *laughs.*)

EMPRESS. Run along, Livenbaum, we're discussing family matters.

LIVENBAUM. I'm not to see her?

EMPRESS. You'd only insist on giving me your opinion and you're never right about anything. *(Giving* LIVEN-BAUM *fur piece)* Go and find this Bounine you hanker after.

(LIVENBAUM *crosess to front door.*)

You may get the blow but I'll be surprised if he gives you the kiss.

(LIVENBAUM *bobs perfunctorially and* PAUL *follows and closes front door behind her.*)

PAUL. Does Anastasia know you are here?

EMPRESS. I believe the lady has been notified.

PAUL. *(Crossing down Left Center)* Please, I beg you, don't make up your mind until you meet her.

EMPRESS. They've gone out of their way to put my back up. Look at that photograph, the eagles on the frame, the servants' liveries—

PAUL. Yes, I agree it's overdone, but—

EMPRESS. If your Anastasia were genuine she'd revolt against it.

PAUL. *(Sits Left of* EMPRESS.) Do try and keep your mind open.

EMPRESS. You're gullible, Paul. You always were. You had reached your teens before you stopped believing in Santa Claus.

PAUL. I'm not as easy as you think. The first time I came here it was in no mood of eager expectancy—I was all prepared to denounce and expose. I had heard about

Bounine and his company and thought the whole thing a disgraceful fraud.

EMPRESS. And then came your conversion from prosecutor to disciple. Quite in the manner of that other Paul —the sainted one.

PAUL. *(Rising; to Left Center)* I was on the point of leaving. I'd been shown in here and while I was waiting, I thought of my last visit to Tsarskoie-Selo. I kissed them all goodbye—I was going off to war and the Emperor went with me to the door. We crossed the Marble Parade Hall, the Hall of Catherine the Second, the Portrait Gallery, the Black Cossacks Hall. Behind us everything entered into the shadow, and I felt that it was there—among those shadows—that they should remain—in their fairy palace with the black eagles—and the might ancestors looking down from the walls. And then Anastasia came into the room. Oh, I didn't recognize her immediately. I hadn't made enough allowance for the years or for all she had gone through.

EMPRESS. She answered your questions, I suppose. What do you expect?—Bounine has taught her her lessons.

PAUL. Bounine doesn't know everything.

EMPRESS. There are many sources he can draw on here in Berlin—old friends, old servants, ghosts from our royal past.

PAUL. *(Crossing Center)* It isn't only what she knows, and it isn't the evidence of her wounds—I've told you about those. No, it's more an atmosphere she creates, a quiet assurance, a fineness that you feel is above question.

EMPRESS. You sound as if you've fallen in love with her.

PAUL. I think perhaps I have.

EMPRESS. You're quite mad. I suppose it's only to be expected. Your mother—poor Eudoxia—when your father died, wanted to marry the Pope.

PAUL. She was alway religiously inclined.

EMPRESS. So you're in love with this sleeping beauty?

PAUL. Shouldn't I be? Don't forget, she was to have been my wife. *(Crossing above to Right of settee)* Why, we actually went through a ceremony of our own devising —a child betrothal. She was twelve and I was fourteen. It was held on the Chinese Island.

EMPRESS. And does she recollect it all clearly?

PAUL. She hasn't mentioned anything about it. It seems to be one of her blank spots.

EMPRESS. She doesn't remember a thing like that and yet you still believe in her? Preposterous!

PAUL. I've spoken to the doctors—to Lessing for one— there's no greater authority. He says some degree of amnesia would be almost inevitable. The head wound was a serious one. Bounine tells me that at times the poor dear has complete lapses—

BOUNINE. Bounine! The girl means nothing to him or his friends. She is simply a means of getting their hands on the millions my son deposited in foreign banks.

PAUL. To buy munitions that came too late.

EMPRESS. As usual. The Tsar was like a man riding backwards on a train—he never saw anything until he was past it.

PAUL. Shouldn't we too give some thought to those millions? Money means power and one day a crisis may arise in Russia and they will want us back.

EMPRESS. The Romanovs? Don't delude yourself. The ants are in power, the red ants. Some day ants of a different color may take their place—but they will still be ants.

PAUL. Ants may be crushed.

EMPRESS. You think so? Once when I went with my husband to Samara we saw one of those ant armies on the march. It was a terrifying sight. Animals came screaming from the desert, covered with the creatures and dying as they ran. The dug trenches—my husband helped—he was like that—and they flooded the trenches with water. But the ants never stopped. They flung themselves in millions upon millions so that their floating carcasses might form a bridge for the hordes that followed them. Alexander had said that the Tsar of Russia must not run away from an army of ants—but we ran. We scrambled aboard our train and fled. I learned then that we live in a world in which numbers must be respected.

PAUL. Perhaps you are right. But the blood of those poor murdered innocents cries out for justice. Those sweet girls—that little boy—

EMPRESS. Leave them. Leave them wrapped in the dignity of death.

(ANNA *enters Left Center.*)

PAUL. *(Crossing up Center to Right of* ANNA) Anastasia! Are you feeling better today?

ANNA. Yes, thank you. My cold is almost gone.

PAUL. Dressed like that you make the past come alive. But this is your Grandmamma's moment. Have confidence. *(He exits Left Center.)*

(ANNA *crosses down Center.*)

EMPRESS. Yes, I can see why the other have believed, especially my romantic-minded nephew.

ANNA. I haven't cared whether *they* recognize me or not. But you—don't you know me?

EMPRESS. Where were you born?

ANNA. In Peterhoff.

EMPRESS. Child, no doubt, of Nicholas the Second and Alexandra, his Empress?

ANNA. And *grandchild* of Maria Feodorovna.

EMPRESS. You have taken a long time in coming to comfort my bereavement.

ANNA. I wrote you letters but you never answered. Perhaps you never got them.

EMPRESS. I have received quite a few appeals from resurrected Romanovs. It seems the Bolshevik firing squads were very poor shots.

ANNA. Twice I started out to try and find you—only there were many days when I did not know who I was.

EMPRESS. But now you do? You at least have accepted yourself. How long have you been an actress?

ANNA. As in your own case, Your Majesty, from earliest childhood.

EMPRESS. Yes, to be a Princess is to be an actress—but not necessarily a good one.

ANNA. Perhaps I should have learned to be a better one if the curtain hadn't fallen so early.

EMPRESS. You are being flippant about a subject which you must realize is for me a great personal sorrow.

ANNA. Forgive me, I forgot for a moment you would be regarding that tragedy as more yours than mine. I am trying to keep my courage. But you are making it very hard for me. I have been without love for so long.

EMPRESS. Come, come—have there been no men in your life? I thought the story of your rescue included a Bolshevik guard who had fallen in love with you and who carried you from the shed where the bodies were awaiting burial?

ANNA. Yes, he rescued me and took me to Rumania, but he soon decided that a crazy girl was no great prize.

EMPRESS. A rescue from the very edge of the grave. Years of lost memory in an asylum. Excellent material for melodrama.

ANNA. Long empty days in which the consciousness of living came only through pain. That's hardly melodrama, Grandmamma.

EMPRESS. Did I give you permission to call me that name?

ANNA. (*Turning away Left*) I'm sorry, it slipped out. I will try to guard my tongue.

EMPRESS. You think my answer should be to grant you that privilege? A lonely old woman should be glad to hear someone call her "Grandmamma."

ANNA. (*Turning to* EMPRESS) My loneliness has been as bitter as yours.

EMPRESS. You ask me for recognition—for love, and you do it well—your eyes are moist, your voice full of feeling. But I can only reply that the love you beg for belongs to one who is dead. You have chosen to deck yourself in the robes of a spectre, Mademoiselle, and so doing,

have managed to win endorsement from a few poor sentimentalists, dreamers, self-deceivers—but I am none of
those things. The shell that was once my heart is not
easily pierced.

ANNA. And so you thrust me from you? I was told you
would ask me difficult questions. But you are not inter-
ested enough to ask me *any*. (*Crosses Left to chair above
table.*)

EMPRESS. Oh, I was going to catechise you, was I?
That is what your business associates told you?

ANNA. They mean nothing to me—these men. Nor the
millions about which they dream.

EMPRESS. But they've told you about those millions?
ANNA. Oh yes, they have told me.

EMPRESS. And did you not say that a Romanov may be
butchered but is not to be bought? That should have
been your answer. For if your blood was truly Romanov
you would not let yourself be made a catspaw by Bounine
and his crew.

ANNA. Tell me to whom this money should be given
and I will give it. Then perhaps you will believe me.

EMPRESS. Easily said. You cannot give the money away
until you have it. And you cannot get it without first
obtaining my recognition.

ANNA. Yes, you are hard. You are showing me your
fighting face, the wounding words, barbed like arrows.
I remember hearing Father say you were the toughest
fighter the family has known since Peter the Great. That
was at the time you and my mother qquarrelled over a
necklace—some emeralds—part of the Imperial treasure
—but you wanted to keep them for your lifetime.

EMPRESS. Who told you this? Oh, but there were plenty
who must have known about it. Rasputin as a beginning.
Alix aired all her grievances to him.

ANNA. You wore them with your last court dress—the
red velvet one with the long train.

EMPRESS. Where did you see my portrait, or did someone describe me?

ANNA. It's strange, I only remember the large outlines or the little details.

EMPRESS. It was the worst of our quarrels—the Winter Palace, my private room, the snow falling outside the double window panes. Alix had herself formally announced by one of the lackeys: "Her Imperial Majesty."—Thought she was going to awe me with a title that had been my own for many years.

(ANNA *crosses slowly to* EMPRESS.)

I was sitting by the fire with my jewel-box on my knees and after that pompous nonsense, I didn't even trouble to get up— I— I don't know why I'm telling all this to you.

ANNA. My father took the side of my mother—they even brought in the Chancellor. They were all lined up against you—but you kept Figgy's jewels.

EMPRESS. How did you learn to call the great Catherine "Figgy"?

ANNA. We always called her that. And sometimes we'd give the same nickname to Marie because she had such an eye for the men. Olga used to tease her and—

EMPRESS. *(Rising; to Right of settee.)* Stop! I forbid it. I forbid you to bandy those names.

ANNA. *(Following)* They are my sisters. I can speak of them if I choose.

EMPRESS. Impostor!

ANNA. *You* call me that?

EMPRESS. Yes, and I want it stopped. If you have any decency I demand that you end this masquerade. I will pay you—give you more than these blackguards will—

ANNA. *(Crossing Left to Right of table)* Go away. Leave me.

EMPRESS. I'm offering you money.

ANNA. Go away, please.

EMPRESS. You're giving up, are you?

ANNA. So it wasn't enough to have suffered all that— the cellar, the asylum, the cruelty—it was also necessary that I should meet you again—like this.

EMPRESS. *(Crossing Center)* Excellent, excellent. The

tragic scene of despair. You're forgetting nothing, are you?

ANNA. How can anyone who has suffered so much have so little heart for suffering?

EMPRESS. I am sorry, Mademoiselle, if your failure to win me over is such a cruel disappointment. Goodbye. *(Crosses toward front door.)*

ANNA. *(Crosses up between* EMPRESS *and door.)* Don't go!

EMPRESS. But you just told me to.

ANNA. Not yet. I'll say nothing more—nothing to try and convince you.

EMPRESS. Then what do you want of me?

ANNA. Just a moment or two longer. *(Drops to her knees.)* Let me touch your dress. Put my hand for a moment in yours. No, just a moment more to hear your voice, to close my eyes, and fancy we are on the terrace of Livadia with the smell of the sea and an echo of laughter from the tennis courts where Father and Olga are playing. You called me little one—"Malenkaia"—it was your own special name for me—you used it for no one else.

EMPRESS. Are you ill?

ANNA. No, it's nothing serious.

EMPRESS. But you have seen a doctor?—a good one?

ANNA. Oh yes. It is kind of you to ask. And I am not after all surprised that you do not recognize me. I know I have changed very much indeed.

EMPRESS. Let me go, please. I must go home.

ANNA. What is strange is that you have altered so little. You still seem to me as you did that day that my finger was pinched in your carriage door and you told me to try not to cry because there were people there and I was the daughter of the Tsar.

EMPRESS. Let me go.

ANNA. Look, it is still not quite straight, that finger. Or, can't you see the difference from the others?

EMPRESS. You are too clever for me. I don't know how

you know these things, but please, Mademoiselle, I am an old woman—I have not the strength—

ANNA. Very well, go if you must. We have met once again—the only two left of our family.

EMPRESS. (*Starting to door*) I shall come back. I will see you once again, Mademoiselle, when my mind is clearer.

ANNA. No, perhaps you had better not come again. You are kind now. You have softened toward me. But later you will get your balance. You will say "It was all acting. She is some sort of cheap little actress hired for money." And it's true, Grandmamma, they did hire me for money. (*She rises.*) I was starving after I ran away from the asylum. I had nowhere to go. (*Crosses down Center.*) I even went down the steps to the canal—perhaps I should not have let him stop me.

EMPRESS. (*At the door.*) Goodbye, Mademoiselle.

ANNA. (*Below settee.*) Goodbye, dear dear Grandmamma —I will try not to be lonely or frightened. Frightened—why did I say that? Where have I said those words before?—Oh yes, I remember—it was on board the *Standart*. I had waked and found a storm raging—the big waves breaking against the hull. I cried out "Grandmamma!" And you came to my cabin. (*She falls to her knees.*)

EMPRESS. (*Crossing down and taking* ANNA *up in her arms*) Malenkaia! Malenkaia! Malenkaia! I couldn't believe it at first. You've come from so far away and I waited and waited and waited. Don't cry—don't say anything—you are warm, you are alive—that is enough. (*Sits on settee.*) I can stand no more for now. Can't you hear how that weary old heart of mine is beating? I must go—but don't be afraid—I shall come back—I need you.

    (*As* EMPRESS *rises,* ANNA *takes hold of her skirt and sits on settee.*)

Let go of my dress. That is what you used to do as a child. Be sensible, Malenkaia. I'll go as I used to—speaking to you as I left the side of your little bed. (*Puts pillow under* ANNA'S *head.*) We will go, tomorrow if you like, to my old palace in Finland. It is still there and still mine. There is a very old man there—our lamplighter. Each evening he goes from one room to another lighting the empty lamps—

(*Starts backing to front door.*) until for him the great dark rooms are ablaze with light. The other servants take no notice—they realize that he is childish. And perhaps that is true of us all—and we are lighting dead lamps to illumine a life that is gone. Goodnight, Anastasia—and please—if it should not be you—don't ever tell me—

(EMPRESS *exits.* ANNA *rises as if in a dream, crosses Center and collapses.*)

PAUL. (*Entering, followed by* BOUNINE) She was magnificent. If the Empress recognizes her— My God! what's happened? (*Crosses down to* ANNA *and cradles her head in his arms.*)

BOUNINE. (*Crossing down to Left of* ANNA) The strain of the interview—

ANNA. Kak nazyvoetsya eta mesta? Ekaterinburg? Ona ochen krasiva ne pravda li?

PAUL. Listen! She's speaking Russian.

(BOUNINE *rises.*)

ANNA. Olga, Tatiana, Marie? Gde Vi? Gde vi? Olga! Tatiana—

CURTAIN

ACT THREE

SCENE: *The scene is the same. Two weeks later.*

It is about eight o'clock at night. A reception is to be held at which the investors in Bounine's syndicate are to be presented to Aanastasia and she, in turn, officially presented to the world.

The set is even more brilliantly lighted. The room is lighted by the large chandelier. On the up Center table is a large bowl of Russian yellow lilies. Down Left is a large throne, rather operatic in appearance, flanked by the two gold armchairs from the previous Act. Behind and on either side of the throne against the Left wall are two gold floor torcheres with candles. The room has been set up as an audience room and six or eight chairs have been placed on the stage, Right side generally facing the throne.

As the Curtain rises, PETROVIN is arranging the footstool in front of the throne. From the front part of the house comes the sound of a group of Russian singers warming up. PETROVIN has just put the cushion on the throne and is down Right admiring the effect.

BOUNINE enters Left Center. He stands in doorway and surveys the room.

BOUNINE. Good. Good. Not quite the Peterhoff throne room—but since that is not available—

PETROVIN. *(Crossing Center)* I've done my best with what I could find.

BOUNINE *(Coming to the edge of the platform)* That throne—where on earth did you get it?

PETROVIN. *(Crossing Left to throne)* Rented for the night.

66

BOUNINE. From whom, may I ask?

PETROVIN. The property department of the Opera. It's from Boris Goudonov.

BOUNINE. *(Crossing down Center and then to down Right)* Couldn't you have got Chaliapin as well?

PETROVIN. *(Crossing Center)* I have nearly as good— a group of Russian singers from the St. Basil's choir.

BOUNINE. Yes. I heard them as I came in. Very effective.

PETROVIN. *(Crossing Right to BOUNINE)* There will be a stream of Glinka, Borodin, Gretchaninov, old Russian hymns. By the time of the presentation they'll be drowning in their tears.

BOUNINE. *(Crossing up Center)* Russian lillies, too! The sentimentalists should be impressed.

PETROVIN. *(Arranging chairs)* They will be ushered into the ballroom when they arrive, and entertained there until the moment comes for them to be presented.

BOUNINE. There's plenty of champagne?

PETROVIN. Of course. And vodka for the more violent patriots.

BOUNINE. *(Crossing to throne)* Now, you'll be dealing with a mass of petty jealousies so the seating arrangements—

PETROVIN. *(Interrupting; crossing to Right of BOUNINE at throne)* I know. I've given Sergei his instructions. The generals and court dignitaries are to have the front seats. The uniforms should make quite a show, despite the bald heads and the weak knees—reds, light blues, yellows—

(BOUNINE *sits on thorne.*)

and the black and gold of the cossacks.

BOUNINE. Quite an historical pageant. And it seems only yesterday it was part of one's everyday life.

CHERNOV. *(Enters up Right Center from cellar. He wears evening clothes but the white scarf still loosely tied about his neck is witness of his upset state. He carries a newspaper. Crossing to Right of PETROVIN)* Have you seen this?

PETROVIN. Where have you been?

BOUNINE. What is it?

CHERNOV. *Die Nachtausgabe.*

BOUNINE. Another of their veiled attacks?

CHERNOV. The veil is off. They call us swindlers. They use the word.

BOUNINE. *(Rising and crossing below Center)* They'll pay for that.

CHERNOV. *(Giving paper to* PETROVIN*)* They say our "so-called royal princess" is a Russian working class girl named Anya Bronin. They say that she is selfdeceived, not quite responsible and that we imposed on her simplicity. *(He crosses to front door.)* They refer to her as our "innocent victim."

(PETROVIN *gives paper to* BOUNINE.)

BOUNINE. *(Sits Right Center chair.)* It's that doctor friend of hers speaking.

CHERNOV. *(Looking out front door)* Obviously.

PETROVIN. *(Crossing above and to Right of* BOUNINE*)* That lame fellow? Why didn't we deal with him the day he came here?

CHERNOV. *(Closing door and crossing to Left Center on platform)* Deal how? He wasn't the kind—

PETROVIN. *(Interrupting)* I don't mean money. It would have been easy to fake an accident. He was hanging about outside for some time.

BOUNINE. Whatever doubts may be raised by this article will mean nothing when weighed against the endorsement of the Empress. *(He puts paper down on chair Right Center.)*

CHERNOV. *(Crossing down Left Center)* Possibly not— so long as you can be sure the Empress is coming.

PETROVIN. The croaker again!

BOUNINE. He invites bad luck.

CHERNOV. *(Crossing to Left of* BOUNINE*)* The bad luck came when you allowed Prince Paul to cart the girl off to Haraldeberg.

BOUNINE. Allowed? How could I stop him? He claimed the right as her fiancé.

PETROVIN. He said the Empress insisted on having her with them.

CHERNOV. You don't know what may have happened. What guarantee have we that even Anna will be here tonight?

BOUNINE. One that is outstanding in the case of a woman—she has had three fittings on the dress she is to wear.

CHERNOV. Did the Empress accompany her to these fittings?

PETROVIN. *(Crossing Left to stool in front of throne)* No, Worth's woman say that she was alone. But she came in the Empress' car.

BOUNINE. *(Rising)* I call that most reassuring.

    (CHERNOV crosses up Right to stove and sits on chcair below stove on platform.)

(BOUNINE crosses to Left Center.) How is the dress?

PETROVIN. A dream in white and gold. Wait till you see it.

BOUNINE. And the tiara?

PETROVIN. It's there on the table.

    (BOUNINE goes to table up Center, picks up tiara box.)

I kept it for you to pass on. *(He sits on stool.)*

BOUNINE. *(Opening box)* Yes, it looks quite impressive.

PETROVIN. They're paste, of course—but good paste. They'd deceive any eye except a jeweler's. And we have none of those among our guests.

BOUNINE. *(Crossing down Left Center with tiara box)* Yes, our fortunes are on the turn. You may still have a chance of fulfilling your destiny as a painter, Piotr.

PETROVIN. And you will be able to restore your stable of race horses—not to mention your even more attractive stable of mistresses.

BOUNINE. I shall go to America. It's the only country left with a proper respect for wealth. *(Crosses up Center and puts tiara box back on table.)*

CHERNOV. You are true Russians, both of you. Realities never bother you for long.

(BOUNINE *crosses Right Center on platform.* SERGEI *KNOCKS; enters front door.*)

SERGEI. Pardon, Excellency. Counsellor Drivinitz would like to have a word with you.

(PETROVIN *and* CHERNOV *rise.*)

BOUNINE. Tell him to come in.

(DRIVINITZ *enters. He is carrying a newspaper.* BOUNINE *picks up paper from chair.*)

DRIVINITZ. *(On platform.)* Have you seen this article?
BOUNINE. Good evening, Counsellor. You are early.
DRIVINITZ. I am speaking of that paper—this article. What do you make of it?
BOUNINE. The work of a Bolshevik agent.
DRIVINITZ. *(Crossing down Center)* General Martoff phoned the newspaper office. They say they have proofs.
BOUNINE. Of course they have proofs—manufactured in Moscow. The pitiful thing is that a group of White Russians whose purses and hearts are both concerned should be so blind as not to see through this attack.
PETROVIN. *(Crossing to Left of* DRIVINITZ) As against this attack, there stands the Romanov family.
DRIVINITZ. True—if they really are backing your claimant.
BOUNINE. *(Taking paper from* DRIVINITZ) Of course they are backing her. And now, with that disposed of, let me tell you something of importance. The Tsar's Swedish bankers will be here tonight.
CHERNOV. *(Crossing down Right)* What?
BOUNINE. Oh yes, I haven't told you, have I? Counsellor Krafting and Count Stromberg are coming.

CHERNOV. Really. *(To* DRIVINITZ.) the heads of the Svenska Handel Bank.

PETROVIN. *(Crossing Right between* BOUNINE *and* CHERNOV) How wonderful!

DRIVINITZ. Yes, but what if they read this article?

BOUNINE. Oh, that won't affect them. They are most favorable disposed towards us. I just spent an hour with them in their suite at the Adlon. The old Empress still carries weight in Scandanavia, and the romance of the reunited sweethearts, as the Count remarked, is a page out of Hans Christian Anderson. *(He hands paper back to* DRIVINITZ.)

PETROVIN. You must admit, sir, that Prince Bounine has managed things very well indeed.

DRIVINITZ. *(Crossing up Left Center on platform)* Well, I will go back and stop General Martoff from up-setting any more people.

(BOUNINE *crosses Center on first step.* CHERNOV *crosses up Right on platform.* PETROVIN *crosses up Center to Left of* BOUNINE.)

Ah, that reminds me. I am having a little trouble over the order of presentation. *(He takes list from pocket)* There is a dispute as to whether precedence should be governed by rank or by the amount each one has subscribed to the fund.

BOUNINE. *(Takes list, crosses on platform, gives it to* PETROVIN.) Is that your list? Give it to me, and I will look it over and advise you.

VARYA. *(Appears in Left Center doorway.)* Pardon, Excellency, but Her Imperial Highness is here.

BOUNINE. Here? Alone?

VARYA. She came in through the garden entrance.

BOUNINE. Quite right. *(Explaining to* DRIVINITZ) Otherwise she might have met some of our guests pre-maturely. *(To* VARYA.) Tell Her Highness I wish to speak with her.

VARYA. Yes, Excellency. (VARYA *exits.)*

DRIVINITZ. And the Empress?

BOUNINE. *(Crossing to* DRIVINIZ) Her Majesty will be coming later.

DRIVINITZ. I suppose the choir will start the anthem the moment she arrives?

BOUNINE. *(Shooing* DRIVINITZ *out front door)* The choir has its instructions.

DRIVINITZ. Yes, of course. *(He exits.)*

PETROVIN. *(Crossing down Right Center between the chairs)* Why did she come alone? I thought they would all arrive together.

BOUNINE. *(Crossing down Right between* PETROVIN *and* CHERNOV) It's just as well. This way we have a chance to find out—

ANNA. *(Enters up Left Center. On platform. Her manner is calm and self-assured. She seems to have fully recovered.)* You wished to speak to me?

(PETROVIN *sits in chair Right Center.)*

BOUNINE. Good evening, Anna. You showed good judgment in coming on ahead of the others. There are matters to discuss.

ANNA. Oh?

BOUNINE. This is an important night.

PETROVIN. The night of nights.

ANNA. *(Crossing down Left Center. With a faint smile.)* The night I am to be presented to my people.

CHERNOV. *(Crossing to Right of* ANNA) Did you make any slips while you were staying at Haraldeberg?

ANNA. Slips?

CHERNOV. Mistakes, blunders.

ANNA. I'm afraid I can't say. I was ill—in a delirium.

CHERNOV. So you might have said anything?

ANNA. *(Moving Left)* Yes, anything.

BOUNINE. *(Crossing Center)* But surely nothing that could have shaken their faith in you?

ANNA. *(Crossing to above throne)* I really don't know.

BOUNINE. *(Crossing to Right of* ANNA) But the Empress is coming here to support you?

ANNA. *(Circling to Left of throne)* I can only repeat. I don't know.

BOUNINE. But, my God! You can't say a thing like that as if it were a matter of no importance. Without her, we are lost.

PETROVIN. *(Crossing down Left, sitting in chair below throne)* Surely there would have been some indication. How was she dressed?

ANNA. Tonight, as always—faultlessly.

BOUNINE. And jewels?

ANNA. *(Crossing below throne to Center between CHERNOV and BOUNINE)* No, she was wearing no jewels.

BOUNINE. *(Crossing to ANNA)* Your complacency is maddening. I don't know if you still believe you are Anastasia—but if the Empress doesn't come here, you'll be alone in that idea.

CHERNOV. *(At Center, showing paper)* There has been an attack in one of the evening papers.

ANNA. *(Crossing Right Center below chairs)* Yes, I saw it. The Empress showed it to me.

CHERNOV. She showed it to you?

PETROVIN. *(Crossing below CHERNOV to ANNA)* What did she say?

ANNA. *(Crossing Right to look at ikons)* Nothing. She merely watched my face as I read it.

BOUNINE. *(Crossing Right below PETROVIN to ANNA)* But what of her attitude toward you? Tell us of that.

ANNA. Her Majesty has shown me great kindness. Owing to her care, I am quite well again.

BOUNINE. Well, that is encouraging.

PETROVIN. *(Sitting Right Center)* She's bound to come. There's her nephew's future to consider. We're getting upset over nothing.

BOUNINE. The Prince will be here, of course?

ANNA. *(Crossing below chairs to Center)* Yes, I think you can count on the Prince.

BOUNINE. Though he may not be enough. I've told you that before. They may say it's the money he's after and that you are his means of getting it.

ANNA. *(Crossing up Center on platform)* Yes, I can imagine many people will think that.

BOUNINE. *(Crosses to table up Center, picks up tiara.)* Now, here is the tiara you are to wear. You must do everything to bolster your self-confidence, so I suggest you think of it as genuine.

ANNA. Genuine? Here?

BOUNINE. On your dressing table you will find a list of the most important people that you will meet tonght, with some personal details jotted against their names. I know you have a photographic memory. Here is the tiara. Take it! Now go!

(She takes it. He crosses Left to bottom of steps.)

ANNA. You do not say "Now go!" to the Tsarina of Russia.

BOUNINE. *(Bows mockingly.)* Pardon—Your Majesty.

ANNA. You speak of my memory. How good is your memory, I wonder?

BOUNINE. What do you mean?

ANNA. It was a lovely autumn morning at Krasnoie. There was a riding contest and Marie and I were both taking part in it. We had Irish hunters given us on our birthdays. You helped me mount and holding my hand, said something too personal. I raised my riding whip—

BOUNINE. *(Stepping back)* Ah—!

ANNA. Was it I? If not, how did I learn it? It was not from your books. *(She turns on* PETROVIN *and crosses down to his Left.)* And you, the artist. You saw two candle-flames reflected in my eyes—standing in a dark church in front of the ikons. And—*beneath* the ikons was a bunch of wild flowers that some poor person had placed there.

PETROVIN. *(Awed.)* Yes, that's true!

ANNA. Our Russian yellow lilies and some blue flowers! *(She turns and crosses up Left Center to the door.)*

PETROVIN. *(Crosses up to Right of* ANNA.*)* Yellow and blue. Who could have told you? Did I speak of it?

ANNA. *(In doorway. Gently, with an enigmatic smile.)* Perhaps you did. You must try and remember. *(She exits.)*

PETROVIN. *(Crossing down Center)* Blue and yellow—no one could have told her—

BOUNINE. *(Starting up steps and turning)* It's impossible. And yet—how did she know?

CHERNOV. *(Rising; to* BOUNINE.) The Empress told her—reminding her of things the real Anastasia had repeated.

BOUNINE. Of course.

PETROVIN. *(Crossing down Left)* That explanation may satisfy you—but not me.

BOUNINE. You're a fool. It must be that.

CHERNOV. *(Crossing, between* BOUNINE *and* PETROVIN*)* Let him have his dream.

PETROVIN. *(Crossing up above Right Center chair)* Your argument before was that she couldn't speak Russian. Well, she can speak Russian—we all know that now!

SERGEI. *(Enters front door. Warningly)* Her Imeprial Majesty!

BOUNINE. Thank God!

(All THREE MEN *turn to the door.* CHERNOV, *taken aback and forgetting fora moment to bow, is reminded by seeing* BOUNINE *and* PETROVIN *bent over ceremoniously.* BOUNINE *is Right Center between the two chairs.* PETROVIN *is Right of* BOUNINE *and* CHERNOV *Right of* PETROVIN. EMPRESS *enters, followed by* LIVENBAUM.)

EMPRESS. Ah, the entire syndicate!

(THREE MEN *come out of bow.)*

I think you'd better give me my smelling-bottle, Livenbaum.

(LIVENBAUM *hands her bottle)*

BOUNINE. *(Crossing up on first step)* Your Majesty is early. May I offer that as my excuse for not being at the door?

EMPRESS. Save your apologies. Pomp without power

only makes deposed royalty ridiculous. Is the lady here?

BOUNINE. In her room, Your Majesty.

(BELL rings off up Left.)

(Over his shoulder to PETROVIN.) Go! People are arriving.

PETROVIN. *(Murmuring)* Yes, Excellency. *(He exits front door.)*

BOUNINE. You, too, Chernov!

CHERNOV. Yes, Excellency. *(He does another bow directed at the* EMPRESS, *falls up the steps, and follows* PETROVIN *off.)*

*(*LIVENBAUM *half closes door and peers off during the following.)*

EMPRESS. *(Still on platform.)* I see you school your associates in the old traditions. Your overbearing manner is quite impressive. *(She walks toward throne.)* What is this?—a throne?

BOUNINE. Rented for this evening's ceremony.

EMPRESS. And is it your idea to present a Romanov on a hired throne? And one, unless I am mistaken, made of papier maché?

BOUNINE. *(Crossing down Center)* May I remind Your Majesty that the realities are now in a museum?

EMPRESS. Yes, our actual state robes are to be seen in London at Madame Tussaud's.

BOUNINE. I trust Her Highness will soon be able to provide herself with more suitable furnishings.

EMPRESS. You are thinking of my son's foreign deposits? *(Crosses to* BOUNINE.) I understand you have caused the lady to sign certain documents concerning these monies—their handling and division.

BOUNINE. I admit the share we asked Her Highness to assign us may sound like rather a large sum, but my two associates and I have taken a great deal of trouble

EMPRESS. A great deal of trouble indeed! The impudence!

LIVENBAUM. *(Shocked.)* Oh!

(BELL rings.)

EMPRESS. Did you speak?

LIVENBAUM. *(Still in doorway.)* Such a lot of old friends arriving. To think they're still alive.

EMPRESS. Only half alive—most of them.

(BELL rings.)

LIVENBAUM. Countess Zolinskaya! May I go and embrace her?

(EMPRESS waves her hand impatiently in a gesture of dismissal. LIVENBAUM bobs and exits front door. BOUNINE starts to speak and is silenced by an imperious gesture from the EMPRESS, who crosses down Right.)

BOUNINE. I assume from Your Majesty's attitude that the—the Princess has told you certain things—?

EMPRESS. She told me nothing deliberately, but the night my nephew brought her to me I sat by her bed for many hours—

BOUNINE. She was in a delirium!

EMPRESS. Yes, a delirium whose fires were very illuminating—the monstrous shapes of nightmare, trembling hopes, black despairs, wavering footsteps that led to a canal.

BOUNINE. *(Taken aback.)* A canal?

EMPRESS. A canal where a poor, broken creature met a cynical brute who bargained with her in the coinage of food and shelter.

BOUNINE. *(Dry-throated.)* I see— Your Majesty knows—

EMPRESS. *(Crossing up to Center on platform)* Everything. The whole dirty fraud.

BOUNINE. *(Following)* Fraud, Your Majesty?

EMPRESS. Yes, you planned a fraud, didn't you. What else do you call it?

BOUNINE. *(Crosses on platform Right Center.)* Surely,

Your Majesty, if my friends and I made an error in believing this girl's story, we can hardly be blamed? You yourself accepted her as genuine.

EMPRESS. Just what I expected! As soon as you see that your droshky is being overtaken, you throw your lady passenger to the wolves. *(She crosses to door Left Center.)*

BOUNINE. *(Crossing Center on platform)* I assure Your Majesty it was she who asserted that she was the Tsar's daughter. I was merely asked my opinion as to the truth of the claim.

EMPRESS. And your nimble brain saw at once that here was a splendid chance for exploitation.

BOUNINE. Please, Your Majesty. My two friends and I merely endorsed an illusion. I am sure the girl believes herself to be your granddaughter.

EMPRESS. Undoubtedly. And I have not come to denounce her. You can make of that what you will.

BOUNINE. I am deeply grateful. Might I hope that Your Majesty would extend her benevolence a little further—?

EMPRESS. *(Crossing down Left Center)* Ah! You want my public acknowledgement—

BOUNINE. *(Following)* Think of your nephew! He will share in the Tsar's millions—millions that may otherwise pass to your son's murderers.

EMPRESS. Very cleverly put.

BOUNINE. As to her— *(He indicates* ANNA's *room and backs up Center.)* If we believed, if you believed for a time, what harm is there in making others believe? Your endorsement would be a truly royal gesture.

EMPRESS. So! You ask for my support whether I believe or not? You invite me, Maria Feodorovna, Dowager Empress of Russia, to be one with you and your friends. Kings and Queens are nothing but names. A museum for our symbols of power—a Madame Tussaud's for our clothes—and it is so easy to get rid of us—a bomb or a plebicite does it. But you've made one mistake, Bounine. There is a tradition that is in our blood, at once our royal burden and our royal privilege—we have pride—not in our position—but in the way we behave. *(Crosses toward door up Left Center.)*

BOUNINE. *(Crossing up)* Without Your Majesty's help, I fear—I greatly fear—

EMPRESS. *(Interrupting)* The audience is over. I am through with you, Arcade Arcadievitch Bounine.

(She starts to exit up Left Center as PRINCE PAUL enters front door.)

PAUL. Ah, here you are. *(He bows and kisses her hand.)* How are you, dear grand-aunt?

EMPRESS. *(With satisfaction.)* Feeling better, thank you. *(She exits.)*

(BOUNINE sits down Right.)

PAUL. *(Closing front door and crossing down Right Center)* I glanced in the ballroom as I came by. Where on earth did they dig up all those diamond dog-collars? Those jewelled kokosniks? It's like a medieval danse macabre revived by Stanislavsky. *(He becomes aware of BOUNINE's dejection.)* Is anything wrong?

BOUNINE. I'm afraid so. It seems Her Majesty has refused us her support.

PAUL. But that's impossible. I'm convinced she has no doubts regarding Her Highness. And her whole attitude —she displays real devotion.

BOUNINE. *(Rising)* Then perhaps you may still be able to persuade her. I had best keep out of it.

PAUL. I sincerely hope I can. Your friend, Chernov, was just telling me we are to have two important visitors.

BOUNINE. Yes, it is chiefly because of them—I have just had a thought. The forthcoming marriage made a deep impression on those Swedish gentlemen. If you could decide when the wedding is to take place and make an announcement—

PAUL. Tonight, you mean?

BOUNINE. Yes.

PAUL. And you think the effect—? Yes, I see—

BOUNINE. What of Easter?—our Russian Easter? It's seven or eight weeks away.

PAUL. An excellent thought!—Excellent!

(ANNA *enters up Left Center.)*

(PAUL *crosses up to Right of* ANNA *on platform.)* You look wonderful! *(He kisses her hand.)* Doesn't she, Bounine?

BOUNINE. *(Crossing to Left of* ANNA *and below on first step)* Superb! Are those jewels—?

ANNA. You were going to ask if they were also supplied by your window-dresser. No, they are surprisingly genuine—a gift of my grandmother.

PAUL. She gave them to you?

ANNA. Yes. But I came to tell you she would like to have a word with you when you are free.

PAUL. There is an important matter I would like to discuss with you.

ANNA. Presently. I have been taught that you mustn't keep royalty waiting.

PAUL. Very well. I hear she is in a difficult mood. *(He exits Left Center.)*

(BOUNINE *closes doors after* PAUL *and turns.* ANNA *crosses down Center.)*

BOUNINE. *(On platform.)* He is ready to marry you. He wants to announce the date tonight.

ANNA. *(Crossing Left)* And am I to have nothing to say about it?

BOUNINE. Oh, he'll ask you for your approval.

ANNA. Which, of course, I must give without question?

BOUNINE. *(As* ANNA *moves close to the throne.)* Go on—sit there. Let me see the Galatea I have fashioned out of the mud of the Landwehr Canal. *(He crosses down Center.)*

(ANNA *sits in throne.)*

Magnificent! Too bad you gave the game away. It seems the Empress knows that you are not Anastasia.

ANNA. Really?

BOUNINE. But she has not come here to denounce you. She told me that definitely.

ANNA. That's kind of her.

BOUNINE. *(Crossing to above* ANNA *at throne)* One thing I can't understand, though, is her giving you those jewels.

ANNA. Strange, isn't it?

BOUNINE. You hate me, don't you?

ANNA. You hate people as you love them—-because they matter to you. I don't hate you, Prince Bounine.

BOUNINE. Indeed? Sublime indifference, eh? *(Crosses to front door.)* Not very grateful of Anya Bronin. Well, perhaps before we're finished with each other, that may change. *(He exits.)*

*(*ANNA *rises from throne and moves below Left Center. As* ANNA *turns back to throne there is a sudden COMMOTION in the hall.* ANNA *crosses Center.)*

LIVENBAUM. *(Off.)* I'm sorry—you can't go in there— No, no, no—you cannot go in there—
    *(*SERENSKY *pushes his way through the doors,* LIVENBAUM *preceding him.)*
These are the rooms of the rolay family.

ANNA. *(Intervening)* It's all right, Baroness. This gentleman is a friend of mine.

LIVENBAUM. *(Apologetically.)* He's not dressed, so I thought—

ANNA. Come in, Doctor Serensky.

LIVENBAUM. Oh, a doctor! *(She exits, closing door.s)*

SERENSKY. *(On platform.)* How lovely you look. And how well.

ANNA. *(Crossing up to Right of* SERENSKY*)* How did you get in here, Michael?

SERENSKY. There was no one to stop me. It seems Bounine and his friends are fully occupied in the ballroom.

ANNA. But why are you staying on in Berlin away

from your work? If it is only to beg me to go back with
you—

SERENSKY. I am not going back to Bucharest. I've
made up my mind to that in the last few days.

ANNA. If that is because of me—

SERENSKY. No, even without you, I shall not go back.
I must go to a country where the individual is not de-
graded—where I can be free to work as I will.

ANNA. I am glad. You have so much to give the world.

SERENSKY. It will not be easy to go where no one
knows you. I do not make friends easily.

ANNA. So you would like to take me with you?

SERENSKY. I did not come tonight to speak of my
wants. I am afraid for you here in the hands of these men.
They would stop at nothing.

ANNA. All they plan is to marry me to a Prince, and to
get their hands on my father's millions.

SERENSKYY. Your father?

ANNA. The Tsar.

SERENSKY. You still believe it, don't you. These men
have told you your dream is true and you believe it.

ANNA. They needn't tell me. I know the truth myself.

SERENSKY. *(Following to Left of* ANNA*)* Anya! I cannot bear to see you self-deluded. In Bucharest when you
would tell your wonderful fantasies it didn't matter—

ANNA. I told you things that didn't happen because I
dared not remember what did. But I have faced it now,
to the last horror, to the death of each of those I loved.

SERENSKY. Dreams, Anya—dreams!

ANNA. Do you know why I ran away from you? Because you talked as you are talking now. You made me
unsure. *(Crosses Right Center.)* When you spoke with
such conviction I would say, "Perhaps Michel is right—
perhaps there was a factory explosion in which my head
was injured."

SERENSKY. There was—I remember when it happened.

ANNA. It was the day we arrived in Bucharest. *(She sits
in chair Right Center.)* Tchaikowsky saw it as a likely
excuse to get rid of me and took me to the hospital with

the story that I was one of the factory workers. Then he and his brother went off with what remained of the jewels.

SERENSKY. *(Crossing to* ANNA*)* You told me yourself how the mists would rise about you and everything would become unreal.

ANNA. Yes, and I would be lost, not knowing who I was or from where I had come. It's a terrible feeling, Michael. I can shudder now when I think of it.

SERENSKY. Anya—

ANNA. No, you need not pity me any more. The mists are gone forever.

SERENSKY. And you have awakened to find yourself a royal princess—

ANNA. You understand, it has never mattered whether or not I was a princess. It only matters that I am I, that someone, if it is only one, has held out their arms to welcome me back from death.

SERENSKY. And someone has?

ANNA. Yes. Someone has.

SERENSKY. This Prince of whom you speak?

ANNA. Prince Paul? He was my childhood sweetheart.

SERENSKY. And he accepts you?

ANNA. Yes.

SERENSKY. *(Crossing below to down Right and back to Right of* ANNA*)* So you will have everything—wealth, beautiful surroundings, a sleek luxurious existence. What could I offer you in exchange?—a struggle. But a struggle is life, Anya—to live is not merely to breathe—it is to act.

ANNA. Go on, Michael. Lecture me like you used to. I can fancy I am back in your office smelling the carbolic and looking at the sign on your desk "To do nothing is to be nothing."

SERENSKY. Those days are gone, Anya. Now we are parting—and probably for the last time.

ANNA. "The last time." How sad those words are—

SERENSKY. All I want is to be sure that you are safe and happy.

ANNA. *(Rising)* If we are parting, Michael—

(He takes her in his arms. They kiss and separate.)

PAUL. *(Enters up Left Center. Crossing down Left Center)* I have good news— Who is this gentleman?

ANNA. This is Dr Michael Serensky.

PAUL. Are you one of the guests?

ANNA. He is one of my guests.

PAUL. I see. *(He goes to front door.)*

ANNA. *(Crossing up to* PAUL *on platform)* Where are you going, Paul?

PAUL. To tell Bounine that my aunt is giving us her support.

ANNA. I want you, and everyone else, to know that Dr. Serensky is under my protection. He is to tsay or go as he pleases. Those are my orders.

PAUL. *(Bowing)* Very well. I will tell them.

SERENSKY. *(Crossing up Center on platform Right of* ANNA*)* Thank you, but it will not be necessary. I am going now. I wonder if, perhaps, it is I who have been living with on illusion—a fond illusion named Anya. *(Starts to exit above* ANNA.*)*

ANNA. Wait, Michael— *(Crossing Right and opening door Right Center)* Go out this way. It will be safer. Through here and to the left, down the stairs to the garden.

SERENSKY. *(Crosses to* ANNA *and kissing her hand)* Thank you, Imperial Highness.

ANNA. No, you must not call me that—even if you should some day believe it.

SERENSKY. Do svidanya.

ANNA. Do svidanya.

(SERENSKY *exits Right Center.* ANNA *closes door.)*

PAUL. Who is he?

ANNA. *(Turning)* The sweetheart of a girl named Anya Bronin.

PAUL. Anya Bronin?—Isn't that the name—?

ANNA. *(Crossing Left on platform to below door Left*

Center) In the paper tonight it says it is my name. Supposing it were, would you still love me?

PAUL. *(Crossing to* ANNA *and taking her hand)* But it isn't.

(They BOTH *cross down Left Center arm in arm.)*

ANNA. Bounine says that you wish to make an announcement tonight of our marriage date.

PAUL. He should have left that to me, but if you are agreeable—

ANNA. You feel it will impress the bankers?

PAUL. That is one thing—but the other—

ANNA. Yes, I can see it is a convincing touch. No one would suppose that you would marry a woman who claimed to be your lost sweetheart unless you were quite, quite sure.

PAUL. You know you have completely satisfied me.

ANNA. And so we can make good the promise of our boy and girl bethrothal—the ceremony on the Chinese Island.

PAUL. You've mentioned it at last. You were bound to speak of it and you have.

ANNA. That was to be your final proof, was it?

PAUL. It was a secret between us and your three sisters. No one living could have told you of it because no one knew.

ANNA. No? You, yourself told me the day you brought the Empress to see me. You spoke of it to her. I was standing behind those curtains trying to muster the courage to come in.

PAUL. *(Stepping back with a look at the Left Center door)* My God, what are you saying? And why? Do you want me to believe this is all a trick?

ANNA. But it is tricks that you have asked for, tricks of remembrance. You could find nothing of personality, nothing of character by which to identify me. Animals know their kind by scent, but *(Crossing to Right Center)* it seems I am not endowed with the rare odor of the Romanovs.

PAUL. *(Following)* You're wrong. I recognized you almost at once, and by instinct, if you want to call it that. These "tricks" are merely the proofs I need for those who still have doubts.

ANNA. *(Turning to him)* Such as the bankers?

PAUL. All right—the bankers.

ANNA. *(Sitting in chair down Right)* Supposing there were no bankers, no money? Would you still be sure that I am the girl to whom you pledged your love?

PAUL. *(Sitting on chair Left of* ANNA*)* Of course.

ANNA. Now it is I who ask for proofs. I suggest that we marry without any reference to bankers or bank-accounts—that we make no claim for this money—that we work for our living, both of us.

PAUL. But why? Why should we?

ANNA. You don't fancy the idea?

PAUL. It makes no sense. Why be poor when you can just as easily be rich?

ANNA. Poor people have one advantage. When they are loved they know it is for themselves.

PAUL. I refuse to take that remark seriously.

ANNA. I'm sorry, Paul—your heart belongs to a young girl who is dead. I may be your childhood, Paul, but I am not your love.

PAUL. Ours was a beautiful childhood because you were part of it.

ANNA. And now you would like to have it back, only with different toys?

PAUL. Our life can once again be gay and charming. Only now we must act. This is a moment of crisis.

ANNA. True, a crisis for the Bounine enterprise, but also a crisis for me. I hoped you would help me solve it— and I think you have.

PAUL. You're talking in riddles, but you're very sweet.

(EMPRESS *enters Left Center.* ANNA *rises, crosses up Center to Right of* EMPRESS. PAUL *rises, crosses*

Right, below ANNA'S *chair and circles to above it on first step.)*

EMPRESS. Well, I have had my half hour alone with my thoughts. It is what my husband always insisted on before he would render a decision.

PAUL. This decision has made me, and I hope Anastasia too, very happy. *(Crossing to front door)* And now I will go and tell the others the good news. *(He exits.)*

EMPRESS. "The others"—Bounine. But much as I hate giving him my support there could be no question of my deserting you.

ANNA. I know that.

EMPRESS. So—if you want these millions, this high position , this royal marriage—

ANNA. The one thing in it all that I would want—is you.

(MUSIC.)

EMPRESS. That you already have. Listen, they are starting the music. You must be getting ready for your audience.

ANNA. In my crown of paste.

EMPRESS. You should be wearing Figgy's emeralds. Take them.

ANNA. Oh, no. Never, never.

EMPRESS. They are yours by right.

ANNA. You have already given me so much. You have given me my sanity, my desire to live. *(Crosses down Center to Right.)*

EMPRESS. *(Crossing down to below chair Right Center)* Very well, but now you must go and get ready. I shall sit by your side when you receive them. I had a struggle with my silly pride but it is put away in my pocket.

ANNA. No, keep your pride, dear, dear Queen Grandmamma.

EMPRESS. *(Sits.)* That is what you used to call me. Now it is only Grandmamma.

ANNA. *(Kneeling at* EMPRESS' *Right)* If there had never been a Queen before, my darling, they would have had to call you one.

EMPRESS. What will happen after tonight? You will not go on here with these men?

ANNA. No, that is finished. The life they would have me lead, surrounded by that pathetic band of exiles— Listen to that music, Grandmamma—the past, always the past.

EMPRESS. The past was strangely beautiful.

ANNA. Yes, the figures move gaily, charmingly; they sing, they dance, they laugh, but behind them hangs a painted backdrop—a cellar in Ekaterinburg.

EMPRESS. I have tried to live as if that horror had never been. I have places set at the table for my dear ones and talk to them as if they were there. I say, "Take that chair, Nicky" and he takes it. "Three lumps, Tatiana? You'll get fat if you eat too many sweets and then the English prince won't want to marry you." Livenbaum thinks I'm quite mad.

ANNA. No one could blame you for living with your dear phantoms. But so much of my life, even from the beginning, has been spent in a shadow world— I want to work, I want to live. And who knows? Perhaps I shall find the things out of which other women make their happiness.

EMPRESS. I understand— Oh, dear, there are tears in my eyes.

ANNA. It was the music.

EMPRESS. Was it?

ANNA. I feel that I should like to put my arms about you and cry with you, but I remember what you told me when I crushed my finger: "Princesses must never be seen to weep."

EMPRESS. True. There's the anthem. *(She rises to Left Center and faces front doors.)*

ANNA. *(Rises; to above* EMPRESS' *chair.)* Does it mean anything any more?

EMPRESS. It still sets my blood tingling as it did when

the imperial bands of the Guards played it in the square outside the Winter Palace.

ANNA. (*Crossing to door Left Center*) I remember.

EMPRESS. (*A deep curtsey.*) "God preserve our noble Empress."

(ANNA *exits.* EMPRESS *looks after* ANNA; *turns Center and crosses slowly Right to chairs.*)

LIVENBAUM. (*Enters front door and crosses to Left of* EMPRESS.) Oh, it's wonderful. Glorious. Prince Paul has told them that you endorse Her Highness. They are all at fever heat.

EMPRESS. Your brooch is undone.

LIVENBAUM. Is it? Oh thank you. (*Crossing excitedly toward front door—back to Right on platform*) Prince Bounine is having difficulty holding them back. They want to come storming in here.

(PAUL *enters, followed by* BOUNINE. LIVENBAUM *crosses down Right.*)

PAUL. (*To Right of* EMPRESS.) It's a complete triumph. They're all laughing and crying.

BOUNINE. (*Crosses down Left Center.*) Yes, the opposers are beaten and the doubters silenced.

EMPRESS. (*Sitting Right Center*) All the doubters? Does that include yourself, Bounine?

PAUL. Isn't Anastasia ready? They are clamoring to see her.

EMPRESS. She is in her rooms.

PAUL. (*Turning to* BOUNINE) We must ask her not to delay.

BOUNINE. (*Crossing to front door*) Yes, now is the moment when the enthusiasm is at its height. (*Calling off*) Varya, Varya!

VARYA. (*Enters front door and closes doors.*) Yes, Excellency?

BOUNINE. Why aren't you up there with Her Highness?

VARYA. She said she would ring if she wanted me.
BOUNINE. Go tell Her Highness we are waiting.

(VARYA *exits Left Center.*)

LIVENBAUM. *(Crossing to Center and bowing)* May I
see if I can help?
EMPRESS. If you like.

(LIVENAUM *exits Left Center.* BOUNINE *crosses Left and
leans against wall, down stage of front door.*)

PAUL. *(Taking* EMPRESS' *arm and escorting her to
chair above throne)* Shall we take our places? I hope all
this excitement doesn't prove too tiring for you.
CHERNOV. *(Entering Left Center)* The Swedish bankers are ready to accept Her Highness' claim without
further question.
PAUL. *(Crossing to chair below throne)* Splendid.
BOUNINE. *(Having closed door Left Center, crosses
over to* CHERNOV.) London can't hold back after that.

(VARYA *enters Left Center with white dress.*)

BOUNINE. My God, what has happened.
VARYA. *(On steps.)* She has gone.
BOUNINE. Gone?
PAUL. Gone where?
EMPRESS. I knew it. She didn't tell me but I knew it!
BOUNINE. *(Crossing halfway down steps)* Where has
she gone? Does your Majesty know?
EMPRESS. *(Takes dress.)*
(VARYA *exits Left Center.*)
It will do you no good to go after her. She won't come
back. She will never come back.

(BOUNINE *exits up Right Center.* CHERNOV *opens door
for him and remains on Right of door.*)

PAUL. *(Crosses to* EMPRESS.) Why has she done this?
What is it she wants?
EMPRESS. To find life—her real life.

PAUL. *(Crosses to chair Right Center.)* Why? I don't understand—that man who was here just now?

EMPRESS. *(Crossing and putting dress on throne)* Perhaps, I do not know.

(PAUL *sits Right Center.*)

BOUNINE. *(Entering from up Right Center and crossing down to Right of* EMPRESS, *followed by* PETROVIN) She has gone. I'll phone the police and have her stopped— If you will say she is suffering a mental derangement—

EMPRESS. Yes—it's in our hands now!

BOUNINE. *(Crossing Left of* PAUL) Your word will be enough. You are her fiancé.

EMPRESS. What do you say, Paul? Would you send her back to the asylum?

PAUL. No.

BOUNINE. *(Crossing above* PAUL *and to his Right)* There are ten million pounds at stake. Ten million—

PAUL. *(Rises; to Left of chair.)* I said no.

EMPRESS. The royal tradition has beaten you, Bounine. I had a feeling that it would.

(LIVENBAUM *appears in front doorway.*)

BOUNINE. *(Sitting down Right)* The royal tradition. The mad Romanovs!

EMPRESS. Well, I am going home. *(She crosses up on platform.)*

(PAUL *holds out his hand and she takes it.*)

You wanted her as she was, keep her as she was, a yellowing photograph of a girl in a white pijue dress waving goodbye from the bridge of the Chinese Island— Come, Livenbaum.

(EMPRESS *opens front door and exits.* LIVENBAUM *and* PAUL *follow slowly as*

CURTAIN

ANASTASIA

PROPERTY PLOT

ACT ONE

On crate down Right:
Vodka bottle, half-full
Brandy bottle, full
3 glasses, juice-size
Box of candy
Matches
Ashtray
Cigarettes
On floor below crate D.R.: Vodka bottle, empty
Leaning against crate D.R.:
2 small paintings, 1 upstage, 1 on stage
Against wall on steps above crate D.R.:
Large painting
Large tapestry
On crate U.R.:
3 photo albums with pictures
2 file drawers
1 pack of books tied with rope
On floor R. of crate U.R.:
2 packs of books tied with rope
Chair R.C.: Lady's fancy hat hanging on chair back
Wall U.C.:
Poster on which is a life-size figure in full court dress
with crown with the legend:
PA3MERbi ¢nrypbi ENB AHACTACNN
Bronze crucifix L. of poster
Photo of real Anastasia in court dress, age 15
Floor U.C.: Jar of paint brushes L. of poster

Hall off U.L.:
   Large landscape facing stage R. covered with cloth
Window seat D.L.:
   1 file darwer with cards
   2 book files
On crate D.L.:
   Circulars in Russian with pictures of Anastasia
Table L.C.:
   Circulars
   Typewriter (1925)
   Ledger
   Gooseneck lamp
   Ashtray
   Matches
   Cigarettes
   Book index file
   Small time book
Off Left:
   Pencil, pen, pince-nez, watch and chain (Chernov)
   Cigarette case, full; lighter, watch and chain (Bou-
      nine)
   Pistol, matches (Petrovin)

CHANGE

Move:
   Tapestry against R. wall to hang on wall over gold
      sofa off U.C.
   Large painting against R. wall to hang on wall in
      hall off U.L.
Note:
   In order to save time ,the panels D.R. and U.C. are
      removed and the panels with ikons substituted
      for Acts II and III

ACT TWO

Wall D.R.:
   Numerous ikons
   Framed picture of the Tsarevitch

On cabinet D.R.:
> Bronze horse
> 2 full decanters
> 1 bottle Brandy
> 1 bottle Vodka
> 5 Brandy glasses
> 1 Vodka glass
> Cigarette box with cigarettes
> Matches

Wall U.C.:
> Ikons over U.C. table
> 1 ikon over cellar door

Table U.C.:
> Vase with tall blue flowers
> Matches
> Ashtary

Door U.C.: Drapes on traveller
Wall L.: 1 ikon over ikon light
Window D.L.: Long draperies, ornate
Table D.L.:
> Pen and ink set
> Candelabra
> Folding ikon
> Picture frame ikon
> Ashtray
> Matches

Table R.C.:
> Photograph album
> Cigarette box with cigarettes
> Matches
> Photo (8 x 10) of Russian royal family in gold
> frame with eagles

Settee R.C.: 3 cushions
Off U.R.:
> 2 ashtrays, lighted cigarette (Sergei)
> Glass of tea (Petrovin)
> Silver tray with powder box, serviette, mirror, comb
> brush (Sergei)

Glass of tea (Varya)
Pillbox with pills (Chernov)

CHANGE

Move:

Gold sofa off U.L. to off U.C.
Red sofa R.C. to off U.L.
Chair U.C. Left of table to R.C.
Chair U.C. below stove to R.C.
Armchairs L. and R. of table stet

Center: U.C. table between doors

ACT THREE

Table U.C.:

Bowl of yellow lilies
Ashtray
Matches
Leather box with tiara

Throne D.L.: Red cushion

Off R.:

Newspaper (Chernov)
Lighted cigarette (Petrovin)

Off U.C.: Anna's white gown—end of Act (Varya)

Off L.:

Newspaper, list (Drivinitz)
Smelling-salts bottle (Livenbaum)

ANASTASIA

COSTUME PLOT

Anna

Act I: Grey shawl; long-sleeved black sweater; brown skirt; brown shirt; long brown wool stockings; carpet slippers.

Act II: Lavender dress with shoes to match; handkerchief; black hair ribbon; white middy blouse; navy wool pleated skirt; black cotton stockings; black shoes with strap.

Act III: Brown fur hat; two-piece tan suit with cape; brown bib, brown velvet bag; brown gloves; tan shoes. White gown embroidered with gold; white shoes; necklace and earrings.

Empress

Act II: Black hat with veil; sable fur piece black wool suit; black jabot; high black shoes with spats; black gloves; umbrella.

Act III: Black satin gown; black shoes; long black gloves; black satin evening bag; black tiara with long veil; emerald necklace.

Bounine

Act I: Black fur hat; black fur-lined overcoat; black gloves; blue-grey business suit with ribbon on lapel; shirt; tie; stickpin; black shoes with spats.

Act II: Striped trousers; black waistcoat; black coat with lapel ribbon; ascot; shirt; wing collar; black shoes with spats; overcoat (Act I).

Act III: Black Cossack uniform; coat; breeches; black boots; belt with dagger; medals; decorations.

Chernov

Act I: Dark pin-stripe suit; grey hat; salt-and-pepper overcoat; black shoes; shirt; tie; pince-nez.

Act II: Black shoes with spats; striped trousers; morning coat; grey waistcoat; ascot; shirt; wing collar.

Act III: Full dress; white scarf; hat and coat (Act I).

Petrovin

Act I: Short overcoat; brown scarf; black Russian blouse; black trousers; brown shoes; rope belt.

Act II: Long morning coat; grey waistcoat; striped trousers; grey four-in-hand; shirt; wing collar; black shoes with spats.

Act III: Full dress.

Drivinitz

Act I: Opera cloak; black homburg; cane; grey gloves; striped trousers; black waistcoat; black coat; shirt; wing collar; ascot; black shoes with spats.

Act III: Full dress.

Serensky

Act II: Old trench-coat; brown suit; shirt; tie; brown shoes; cane.

Act III: Same as Act II. Change shirt and tie.

Prince Paul

Act II: Black homburg; yellow gloves; black overcoat with fur collar and cuffs; striped trousers; beige waistcoat; black coat; striped shirt; white collar; grey tie with stickpin; black patent leather shoes with spats.

Act III: Full dress; red sash; sunburst order; decoration around neck.

Sergei

Act I: Green chauffeur's uniform; black puttees; black shoes.

Act II: Gold braid footman's uniform; coat; vest; knee breeches; lace bib; long-sleeved undershirt; white stockings; black pumps with buckle.

Act II: Same as Act II.

Varya

Act I: Green shawl; Russian blouse; rust skirt; rope belt; black cotton stockings; black slippers.

Act II: Black maid's cap; black uniform with white collar and cuffs; white apron; black stockings; black shoes.

Act III: Same as Act II.

Sleigh Driver

Act II: White wig and beard; long green coat; wide belt; old trousers; black boots.

Charwoman

Act II: Figured shawl; black blouse; black underskirt; black overskirt; brown boots.

Livenbaum

Act II: Grey wig; black plush coth coat with beaver collar and cuffs; green wool skirt; black hat with plume; high shoes; alligator bag; black gloves; earrings; necklace.

Act III: Beaded dress; long white gloves; beaded bag; brown shoes; black stockings; tiara; earrings; necklace; brooch.

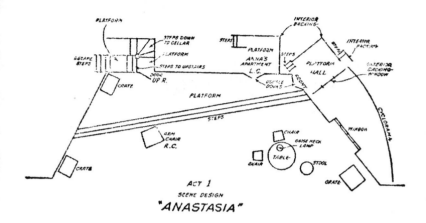

ACT 1
SCENE DESIGN
"ANASTASIA"

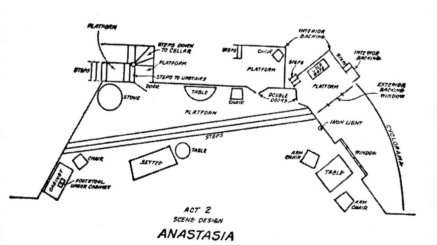

ACT 2
SCENE DESIGN
ANASTASIA

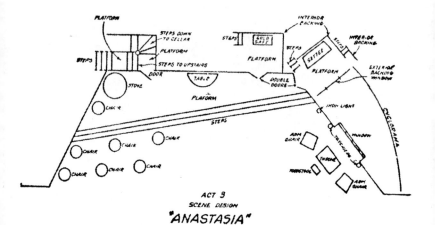

ACT 3
SCENE DESIGN
"ANASTASIA"